Urban Waterfronts: Advancing Climate Resilience, Sustainable Development, Nature-Based Solutions, Smart Infrastructure, Circular Economy, and Inclusive Design

Copyright

Urban Waterfronts: Advancing Climate Resilience, Sustainable Development, Nature-Based Solutions, Smart Infrastructure, Circular Economy, and Inclusive Design

© 2025 Robert C. Brears

ISBN (eBook): 978-1-991368-41-6

ISBN (Paperback): 978-1-991368-42-3

Published by Global Climate Solutions

First Edition, 2025

Cover design and interior layout by Global Climate Solutions

Table of Contents

Introduction

Urban waterfronts have always held a unique place in the evolution of cities. They have been the gateways of commerce, the meeting points of cultures, and the landscapes where communities have drawn sustenance and meaning. From the early settlements clustered around rivers and seas to the great industrial harbors that powered global trade, waterfronts have shaped the trajectory of human development. Yet, in the twenty-first century, they are being reimagined once more, as climate pressures, social demands, and ecological concerns transform how these spaces are valued and designed.

The challenges facing waterfronts today are profound. Rising seas, intensifying storms, and unpredictable flooding place immense stress on built environments along the water's edge. Industrial legacies have left behind contaminated sites and disconnected neighborhoods. Meanwhile, the pressures of urbanization bring competing demands for housing, commerce, recreation, and ecological preservation. The waterfront is no longer a neglected boundary of the city but a dynamic front line where resilience, innovation, and equity must converge.

In response, cities around the world are turning to new strategies that blend ecological restoration, social inclusivity, and technological advancement. Nature-based solutions are gaining prominence, not only for their capacity to buffer climate risks but also for the broader benefits they bring—cleaner water, enhanced biodiversity, and healthier communities. These approaches, combined with adaptive design, innovative planning, and digital technologies, are redefining what it means to live with water rather than against it.

At the same time, urban waterfronts are increasingly recognized as social and cultural spaces that connect people to their heritage and identity. Access, equity, and inclusivity are central to this transformation, ensuring that waterfronts are shared and celebrated by all rather than reserved for a privileged few. Economic opportunities also continue to evolve, from the traditional roles of trade and transport to emerging blue economy initiatives, tourism, and creative industries. The waterfront remains an engine of prosperity, but it is now tasked with generating growth that is sustainable and fair.

This book explores the future of urban waterfronts through nine chapters that each address a critical dimension of their transformation. It examines historical trajectories and contemporary pressures, the integration of nature-based and technological solutions, the roles of governance and design, and the possibilities for shaping equitable and sustainable futures. The intention is not to prescribe a single model, but to present the frameworks and principles that allow for adaptation across diverse contexts.

Waterfronts embody the spirit of possibility. They are edges that can unite rather than divide, spaces where natural systems and human ambition coexist, and stages where resilience and creativity play out. By understanding their past, acknowledging their challenges, and envisioning their potential, cities can harness the waterfront as a defining arena for twenty-first-century urban life. This book seeks to illuminate the pathways by which urban waterfronts can become living laboratories of resilience, equity, and sustainability for generations to come.

Chapter 1: The Evolution of Urban Waterfronts

Urban waterfronts have long been at the center of human settlement, trade, and cultural life. From ancient harbors that connected civilizations to the industrial docks that powered global economies, these spaces have continuously evolved in response to shifting social, economic, and environmental forces. Once bustling hubs of commerce and industry, many waterfronts later declined under the weight of pollution and disuse. Today, they are being reimagined as vibrant, multifunctional landscapes that integrate resilience, culture, and sustainability. Tracing this historical evolution provides crucial insights into how waterfronts can continue to adapt and shape urban futures in the twenty-first century.

Historical Roles of Waterfronts

Waterfronts have been at the heart of human settlement since the earliest stages of civilization. Rivers, lakes, and seas provided the natural resources and mobility that allowed communities to flourish, offering food, transportation, and access to wider networks of trade. Ancient societies often established themselves at these water edges because they were lifelines of survival, bringing both sustenance and connection. From the banks of the Nile in Egypt to the harbors of Mesopotamia, waterfronts became the stage on which culture, governance, and commerce unfolded. They were not simply functional spaces but symbolic landscapes, embodying both power and identity for the societies that grew alongside them.

As trade expanded, waterfronts grew into central economic hubs. Coastal settlements became harbors where ships exchanged goods across vast distances, fueling the rise of maritime empires. The Mediterranean, with its extensive networks of ports, illustrates how waterfronts supported the growth of complex political and cultural systems. Cities such as Athens, Rome, and later Venice depended on their waterfronts not just for survival but as the foundations of their prosperity. The seafront was the entry point for wealth, technology, and cultural exchange, making these areas the most vital parts of urban life. In Asia, waterfronts along the Ganges, Yangtze, and Mekong rivers supported thriving civilizations, combining agricultural fertility with transport systems that connected rural hinterlands to expanding cities.

Waterfronts also carried cultural and spiritual meaning. In many societies, water was revered as sacred, and waterfronts became places of ritual and ceremony. They were locations for festivals, religious offerings, and symbolic representations of life, death, and renewal. Ancient temples and shrines were often constructed along water edges, integrating the natural rhythms of tides and floods into human expressions of meaning. This cultural role elevated waterfronts beyond the purely practical, embedding them in the collective memory of communities.

Over time, the functions of waterfronts diversified further as military considerations came into play. Control over a port or a river mouth often meant control over a territory. Fortresses, naval bases, and defensive walls were frequently constructed at the water's edge, reinforcing the importance of waterfronts as strategic sites. Naval power became a determining factor in the fortunes of empires, and the ability to command waterfronts often dictated the rise and fall of regional dominance.

Waterfronts also became sites of identity, shaping the social and political life of cities. Marketplaces and gathering spots were often located along piers and harbors, where the constant flow of goods and people created spaces of exchange and interaction. These areas were melting pots where merchants, sailors, and local residents came together, making waterfronts among the most cosmopolitan and dynamic parts of any city. The diversity of people and products that converged on waterfronts fostered cultural hybridity and innovation, with influences spreading from one society to another.

By the time of early modernity, waterfronts had become firmly established as urban focal points. They were both economic lifelines and cultural mirrors, reflecting the prosperity and ambitions of the cities they served. Palaces, warehouses, and markets were built along riverbanks and coastlines, turning waterfronts into showcases of power, wealth, and prestige. They were at once practical and symbolic, embodying the intersection of survival, prosperity, and cultural expression.

In tracing the historical roles of waterfronts, it becomes clear that they have always been more than just geographic features. They have functioned as vital connectors, sustaining life, supporting economies, and shaping identities. Their significance lies not only in their ability to meet material needs but also in their role as cultural and social anchors of human communities. Understanding these historical foundations provides essential context for how waterfronts continue to evolve in the present, as spaces where economic, cultural, and ecological dynamics intersect.

Industrialization and Its Legacy

The industrial revolution of the eighteenth and nineteenth centuries marked a decisive turning point in the history of urban waterfronts. What had long been spaces of trade, cultural exchange, and community life were rapidly transformed into engines of industrial production and distribution. Cities across Europe, North America, and later Asia reconfigured their waterfronts to serve as gateways for raw materials, manufacturing, and exports. This period embedded new physical, economic, and social legacies that continue to shape waterfronts today.

Waterfronts became synonymous with industry, as factories, warehouses, and shipyards were constructed along rivers and harbors. These sites provided the dual advantage of transport and power, with rivers not only facilitating the movement of goods but also generating energy for mills and machines. Coal, iron, and other raw materials were unloaded directly at the water's edge, minimizing transport costs and maximizing efficiency. The growth of canals, docks, and rail links further reinforced the centrality of waterfronts to the industrial economy, transforming them into heavily mechanized and densely built landscapes.

The expansion of shipping technologies reinforced this transformation. The advent of steamships and later larger steel vessels required deeper harbors, expansive docks, and specialized infrastructure. Waterfronts became dominated by cranes, warehouses, and rail lines, creating highly utilitarian environments focused on efficiency and productivity. These developments reinforced the role of waterfronts as global connectors, linking industrial cities to colonies, markets, and distant suppliers. Cities like London, Liverpool, New York, and Hamburg became industrial giants precisely because of their waterfront infrastructure, while smaller port cities expanded rapidly as global demand for goods grew.

With industrialization, waterfronts also became sites of intense labor activity. The demand for workers to load and unload ships, operate warehouses, and manufacture goods drew thousands of people to waterfront districts. Working-class neighborhoods often grew adjacent to docks and factories, shaping the social and spatial character of entire urban areas. However, these environments were typically harsh, polluted, and overcrowded, reflecting the inequalities of industrial capitalism. Waterfronts became places of both opportunity and exploitation, marked by long hours, dangerous working conditions, and minimal protections for laborers.

Industrial activity brought significant environmental consequences. The very qualities that made waterfronts attractive—proximity to water for transport, energy, and disposal—also made them vulnerable to degradation. Factories discharged waste directly into rivers and harbors, contaminating water supplies and damaging aquatic ecosystems. Air pollution from coal-powered industries and ships filled waterfront districts with soot and smoke, further degrading the urban environment. In many cities, the once vibrant cultural and ecological role of waterfronts was eclipsed by their function as polluted industrial zones.

Despite these challenges, industrial waterfronts symbolized progress and modernity for much of the nineteenth and twentieth centuries. They embodied the power of technology and the wealth of growing cities, serving as visual markers of industrial achievement. The skylines of dockside cranes, warehouses, and smokestacks were symbols of prosperity and productivity, even as they masked the environmental and social costs of industrialization.

The legacy of this era remains imprinted on urban waterfronts today. Abandoned warehouses, derelict docks, and polluted sediments are reminders of the intensity of industrial use. In many cities, industrialization created physical barriers between the city and the water, as access was restricted to workers, ships, and industries. Communities were often cut off from their waterfronts, transforming what had once been shared public spaces into privatized industrial zones. These divisions have persisted long after industries relocated or declined, leaving a complex inheritance for contemporary urban planners and communities seeking to reconnect with their waterfronts.

Industrialization thus redefined the role of waterfronts in ways that continue to resonate. It transformed them into strategic nodes of production and trade, but at the cost of social inequity, environmental degradation, and urban disconnection. Understanding this legacy is essential to grasping the challenges of modern waterfront redevelopment, as cities attempt to reconcile the industrial past with visions of sustainable, inclusive, and resilient futures.

Shifts Toward Post-Industrial Waterfronts

The decline of heavy industry and traditional shipping in the mid-twentieth century marked the beginning of a profound shift in the role of urban waterfronts. The forces that had once concentrated industrial activity along the water's edge—proximity to shipping routes, access to raw materials, and space for warehouses—began to diminish as economies transitioned from manufacturing toward services and knowledge industries. This transformation produced derelict landscapes of abandoned docks, warehouses, and polluted shorelines, yet it also opened the way for reimagining waterfronts as cultural, recreational, and ecological assets. The shift toward post-industrial waterfronts reflects broader changes in the global economy, urban planning, and societal expectations of what waterfronts should represent.

A central driver of this transformation was the technological revolution in shipping, particularly containerization. The adoption of standardized shipping containers in the 1950s and 1960s required larger ports with deeper harbors, expansive container yards, and sophisticated logistics facilities. Traditional waterfront docks located in the centers of cities could not accommodate these changes, leading to their obsolescence. Shipping operations moved to peripheral locations where space was abundant, leaving inner-city waterfronts redundant. Once-thriving docklands and industrial areas were left in decline, producing large tracts of unused and degraded land at the water's edge.

At the same time, economic globalization and deindustrialization reduced the role of heavy industry in many advanced economies. Factories and shipyards that had anchored waterfront economies closed or relocated overseas, leading to job losses and the collapse of local economies that had depended on them. The urban waterfront, once the hub of industrial vitality, became instead a landscape of disinvestment and dereliction. Yet these vacant areas also represented opportunities for reinvention, providing large tracts of centrally located land adjacent to natural and cultural amenities.

Urban planners and policymakers began to recognize the potential of post-industrial waterfronts to support new forms of urban life. Rather than serving as restricted industrial zones, waterfronts could be redeveloped as mixed-use districts that combined housing, commerce, culture, and recreation. This shift reflected changing values in society, as citizens increasingly demanded access to the water for leisure and quality of life. The waterfront was no longer viewed solely as an economic engine but as a shared space where urban residents could live, work, and play.

Cultural and symbolic considerations also played a role in the reimagining of waterfronts. Once associated with pollution, decline, and social marginalization, waterfronts were rebranded as spaces of identity, heritage, and civic pride. Historic warehouses and docks were preserved and adapted for new uses, becoming museums, art galleries, and cultural centers. Public promenades, parks, and plazas were constructed to reconnect people with the water. This cultural shift repositioned the waterfront as a defining feature of urban identity, attracting both residents and visitors.

Environmental concerns further shaped the transformation of post-industrial waterfronts. As awareness of pollution and ecological degradation grew in the late twentieth century, efforts to clean up and restore waterfront environments became central to redevelopment strategies. Former industrial sites were remediated, wetlands and habitats were restored, and new green infrastructure was introduced to manage stormwater and improve resilience. This ecological turn aligned with broader sustainability goals, positioning waterfront redevelopment as a vehicle for both environmental restoration and climate adaptation.

The shift toward post-industrial waterfronts also intersected with broader trends in real estate and urban development. The desirability of waterfront locations for housing and commercial activities drove significant investment and redevelopment, often leading to rising property values and gentrification. While these projects revitalized neglected areas, they also raised questions about equity and access, as long-term residents and low-income communities were often displaced or priced out of newly redeveloped districts. Balancing the economic potential of waterfront redevelopment with the need for inclusivity became a central challenge for cities navigating this transition.

By the early twenty-first century, the post-industrial waterfront had become a global phenomenon. From North America to Europe and Asia, cities reimagined their waterfronts as vibrant, multifunctional spaces that integrated culture, commerce, ecology, and recreation. While the forms and outcomes varied, the underlying theme was the recognition that waterfronts could no longer be defined solely by industry and shipping. They had become places of urban renewal, environmental restoration, and social connection—critical spaces where the aspirations of sustainable and resilient cities could be realized.

The shift toward post-industrial waterfronts thus represents both a response to economic change and a broader redefinition of urban values. Where industrial activity once dominated, today's waterfronts aspire to embody sustainability, inclusivity, and cultural vitality. The challenge now lies in ensuring that these transformations not only generate economic growth but also deliver resilience, equity, and ecological health, setting the stage for the waterfronts of the future.

Emerging Drivers of Waterfront Transformation

The transformation of urban waterfronts in the twenty-first century is shaped by a combination of environmental, economic, technological, and social forces that are redefining the relationship between cities and their waters. No longer confined to their historic roles as industrial or logistical hubs, waterfronts are now viewed as multifunctional spaces that must simultaneously address climate change, support sustainable development, and enhance urban livability. These emerging drivers are creating both opportunities and challenges, compelling cities to rethink how waterfronts can be designed, governed, and integrated into broader urban systems.

One of the most significant drivers is climate change. Rising sea levels, storm surges, and increasingly unpredictable weather patterns place immense pressure on waterfront areas, which are often among the most vulnerable parts of cities. In this context, waterfronts are no longer passive edges but critical frontlines of adaptation and resilience. Investments in flood defenses, nature-based solutions such as wetlands and mangroves, and resilient infrastructure are becoming essential. This shift has elevated the role of waterfronts in climate adaptation planning, turning them into laboratories for innovative responses to environmental risks. The urgency of climate change ensures that resilience is now a central consideration in all waterfront development projects.

Another major driver is the growing emphasis on sustainability and the circular economy. Cities are seeking ways to integrate resource efficiency into waterfront planning, using the water's edge not only as a site for housing and commerce but also as a platform for renewable energy, water recycling, and waste management systems. Waterfronts provide unique opportunities for linking ecological restoration with resource recovery, whether through district energy systems powered by tidal flows or through urban agriculture projects supported by reclaimed water. These developments reflect a broader societal expectation that waterfronts contribute to sustainable urban futures rather than perpetuate extractive or polluting practices.

Economic restructuring also plays a crucial role in waterfront transformation. As traditional shipping and heavy industry have relocated or modernized, the land they once occupied has become available for new purposes. The global economy increasingly revolves around knowledge, services, and creative industries, which thrive in dynamic, attractive urban environments. Waterfronts, with their central locations and aesthetic appeal, have become prime sites for redevelopment into mixed-use districts that combine offices, residential spaces, cultural institutions, and recreational amenities. This economic diversification has turned waterfronts into engines of urban revitalization, attracting investment and boosting competitiveness in global city networks.

Technological innovation further accelerates the reimagining of waterfronts. Digital tools such as sensors, data analytics, and digital twins are transforming how waterfronts are monitored, planned, and managed. Smart infrastructure enables cities to track water quality, manage stormwater, and optimize transportation in real time. Advanced modeling allows planners to test scenarios for flood risk or redevelopment before implementing physical changes. These technologies not only improve efficiency but also enhance resilience by enabling adaptive and evidence-based decision-making. In this way, waterfronts are emerging as testing grounds for digital innovation in urban systems.

Social and cultural dynamics are also reshaping waterfronts. Citizens increasingly demand equitable access to these spaces, viewing them as essential public goods rather than restricted or privatized zones. This shift reflects broader urban movements toward inclusivity, social justice, and community well-being. Waterfronts are being reimagined as shared cultural landscapes, integrating heritage, art, and community identity into their design. As cities become more diverse, the symbolic and cultural role of waterfronts as places of gathering, celebration, and belonging is becoming more prominent. This driver emphasizes that successful waterfront transformation must go beyond physical development to address questions of equity, identity, and inclusion.

Finally, governance innovation is an emerging driver of change. The complexity of waterfront redevelopment requires coordination across multiple levels of government, private investors, civil society, and local communities. Traditional top-down approaches are giving way to more collaborative models that emphasize participation, partnership, and long-term stewardship. This reflects a recognition that waterfronts are not just sites of development but also shared resources whose management must balance diverse interests and future generations.

Together, these emerging drivers underscore the evolving role of waterfronts as integrated, multifunctional spaces at the intersection of environmental resilience, economic opportunity, technological innovation, and social inclusion. The transformation of waterfronts is not driven by a single factor but by the convergence of these forces, which demand holistic and adaptive approaches. As cities continue to navigate these pressures, waterfronts will increasingly define what it means to create sustainable, resilient, and equitable urban futures.

Chapter 2: Climate Change and Urban Waterfronts: Nature-Based Defenses

Climate change is exposing urban waterfronts to intensifying risks from rising seas, stronger storms, and more frequent flooding. Traditional hard defenses, while offering immediate protection, are often costly, rigid, and ecologically damaging. In response, cities are increasingly turning to nature-based defenses that harness natural processes to provide adaptive and regenerative protection. Wetlands, dunes, mangroves, and floodplains absorb wave energy, reduce erosion, and offer critical habitats. Beyond protection, these systems enhance biodiversity, improve water quality, and provide recreational and cultural benefits. By integrating nature into design, urban waterfronts become more resilient, multifunctional, and sustainable in the face of climate uncertainty.

Rising Seas and Flooding Risks

Waterfronts, by their very nature, exist at the intersection of land and water, making them uniquely vulnerable to the impacts of rising seas and flooding. As climate change accelerates, global sea levels are rising at unprecedented rates, threatening the integrity of coastal and riverfront cities alike. For urban waterfronts, which often host dense populations, critical infrastructure, and significant economic activity, the risks associated with sea-level rise and flooding are among the most pressing challenges of the twenty-first century. The scale and complexity of these risks demand both immediate responses and long-term planning, reshaping how cities engage with their waterfronts.

Rising seas are a direct consequence of climate change, driven by the melting of glaciers and polar ice sheets alongside the thermal expansion of warming oceans. Even modest increases in sea levels amplify the risks of coastal flooding, particularly when combined with storm surges and extreme weather events. For waterfront cities, the result is a higher frequency of inundation events that once might have been considered rare. Low-lying neighborhoods, port facilities, and waterfront infrastructure now face chronic flooding, with some areas experiencing so-called "sunny day flooding" during high tides. This normalization of flooding highlights the severity of the threat, undermining both economic activity and community well-being.

The risks extend beyond temporary inundation. Rising seas cause saltwater intrusion into freshwater aquifers, contaminating vital water supplies and damaging agricultural land near waterfronts. Erosion accelerates along shorelines, undermining the foundations of buildings, roads, and protective barriers. In riverfront cities, more intense rainfall and changing river flows compound the risks, leading to both coastal and inland flooding. The convergence of these processes demonstrates that rising seas and flooding risks are not isolated issues but interconnected pressures that affect the entire urban fabric.

Urban waterfronts face heightened exposure because they concentrate essential assets in vulnerable zones. Ports, energy facilities, and transportation networks are frequently located along waterfronts to take advantage of proximity to waterborne trade and power generation. Residential and commercial development has also intensified along waterfronts, attracted by the prestige and amenities of living or working near the water. These patterns of development amplify the risks, as large populations and critical economic functions are placed in harm's way. In many cities, the most valuable and heavily used real estate is also the most vulnerable to rising seas and flooding.

The social implications of rising seas are equally significant. Waterfront flooding often disproportionately impacts low-income communities and marginalized groups, who may live in less-protected areas or lack the resources to recover from repeated losses. Housing insecurity, displacement, and loss of livelihoods are real and growing risks. As flooding events intensify, questions of equity and justice come to the forefront, requiring planners and policymakers to ensure that adaptation strategies do not exacerbate existing inequalities. Protecting waterfronts, therefore, is not simply a matter of engineering solutions but of safeguarding communities and ensuring inclusive resilience.

Cities are increasingly turning to a mix of strategies to address these challenges. Traditional approaches have relied on engineered defenses such as seawalls, levees, and storm surge barriers to protect waterfronts from flooding. While these remain important, their limitations are increasingly apparent in the face of escalating risks. Rigid barriers can displace water elsewhere, creating new vulnerabilities, and are costly to maintain over the long term. As a result, there is a growing shift toward more adaptive and flexible strategies that combine gray infrastructure with nature-based solutions. Restored wetlands, mangroves, and dunes act as buffers against storm surges while also enhancing biodiversity and providing co-benefits for communities. These hybrid approaches recognize the need for resilience strategies that evolve with changing conditions.

At the same time, cities are rethinking land use and development patterns along waterfronts. Some are exploring managed retreat, relocating vulnerable infrastructure and communities to safer ground. Others are adopting design principles that allow for controlled flooding, using open spaces and flexible infrastructure to absorb and adapt to inundation rather than resist it outright. These approaches require long-term vision and careful planning, as the impacts of rising seas will unfold over decades and centuries.

Ultimately, rising seas and flooding risks are transforming how cities perceive and plan their waterfronts. No longer simply desirable real estate or economic gateways, waterfronts are becoming frontlines of climate adaptation, where the success or failure of resilience strategies will have profound consequences. The challenge lies not only in protecting these spaces from immediate threats but also in reimagining them as dynamic, adaptable landscapes that can coexist with water. The urgency of the climate crisis ensures that rising seas and flooding risks will remain central to the future of urban waterfronts, demanding solutions that are innovative, inclusive, and enduring.

Waterfronts as Climate Adaptation Frontlines

Urban waterfronts are increasingly recognized as frontlines in the global struggle to adapt to climate change. Positioned at the delicate boundary between land and water, they are among the first and most visible places where the consequences of rising seas, stronger storms, and unpredictable flooding manifest. Yet, rather than being viewed solely as zones of vulnerability, waterfronts are being reframed as opportunities to experiment with, implement, and scale climate adaptation strategies. Their prominence in urban life, combined with the urgency of climate risks, positions them as pivotal spaces where adaptation is not optional but essential.

The adaptation role of waterfronts is rooted in their exposure. Unlike inland areas, waterfronts cannot ignore the advancing pressures of climate change. Sea-level rise, coastal erosion, tidal flooding, and storm surges directly impact these areas, threatening homes, businesses, and infrastructure. In many cities, waterfronts also host critical facilities such as ports, power plants, and transportation hubs, making their protection a matter of economic security as well as public safety. The need to safeguard these assets has pushed waterfront adaptation to the top of municipal and national agendas, spurring investments in innovative responses that often set precedents for broader urban adaptation strategies.

One of the defining features of waterfront adaptation is its multifunctionality. Unlike single-purpose interventions that provide only flood defense, contemporary adaptation strategies along waterfronts seek to integrate protection with additional ecological, social, and economic benefits. For instance, restored wetlands or mangrove forests can buffer storm surges while simultaneously improving biodiversity, sequestering carbon, and enhancing recreational opportunities for residents. Parks designed as floodable landscapes can absorb excess water during storms but function as vibrant public spaces under normal conditions. These approaches illustrate how adaptation measures along waterfronts can provide layered benefits that strengthen urban resilience across multiple dimensions.

Waterfronts also serve as visible and symbolic arenas for climate adaptation. Because they are highly valued and accessible parts of cities, adaptation efforts implemented at the water's edge are often highly visible to the public and attract significant attention. This visibility can generate momentum for climate action, demonstrating what is possible and building support for broader resilience initiatives. Waterfront adaptation projects can therefore act as catalysts, raising awareness, inspiring innovation, and embedding climate considerations into the urban imagination. Their symbolic role helps normalize adaptation as a necessary and achievable response to climate risks.

Governance plays a crucial role in positioning waterfronts as adaptation frontlines. Effective adaptation requires collaboration among multiple stakeholders, including city governments, national agencies, private developers, community groups, and environmental organizations. Waterfront projects often bring these groups together, fostering partnerships and shared responsibility. In many cases, they also highlight tensions—between development and conservation, private interests and public access, short-term profits and long-term resilience. Navigating these tensions requires innovative governance models that emphasize inclusivity, transparency, and long-term planning. By testing new forms of governance, waterfront adaptation can provide lessons for managing climate risks in other urban contexts.

Equity is another essential dimension. While waterfront adaptation often aims to protect valuable infrastructure and high-profile urban districts, it must also consider vulnerable communities that live along riverbanks, coasts, and flood-prone zones. If adaptation measures prioritize only high-value real estate, they risk exacerbating inequalities by displacing low-income residents or leaving marginalized neighborhoods unprotected. Recognizing this, more cities are embedding equity goals into waterfront adaptation, ensuring that benefits are distributed fairly and that community voices shape decision-making. By addressing both physical risks and social vulnerabilities, waterfronts can embody a holistic approach to climate resilience.

Overall, waterfronts are at the forefront of reimagining how cities coexist with water. They are no longer simply edges to defend but dynamic interfaces where adaptation strategies must be integrated into daily urban life. By combining protective infrastructure with ecological restoration, inclusive design, and participatory governance, waterfronts can demonstrate how cities can adapt creatively and sustainably to a changing climate. As the pressures of climate change intensify, the ability of urban waterfronts to function as adaptation frontlines will be a defining factor in the resilience of cities worldwide.

Integrating Nature-Based Defenses

As waterfront cities confront the growing risks of sea-level rise, storm surges, and flooding, attention is increasingly turning toward nature-based defenses as critical components of adaptation. Unlike traditional gray infrastructure such as seawalls and levees, which often create rigid barriers between water and land, nature-based defenses harness ecological processes to provide flexible, adaptive, and multifunctional protection. By restoring and enhancing natural systems, cities are discovering that waterfronts can serve as resilient buffers while also delivering ecological, social, and economic benefits. This integration of natural and built solutions represents a paradigm shift in how waterfronts are designed for resilience.

At the heart of nature-based defenses is the concept of working with, rather than against, natural processes. Wetlands, mangroves, dunes, and salt marshes, for example, naturally absorb wave energy, reduce erosion, and dissipate storm surges. Their ability to adapt to changing conditions makes them particularly valuable as climate risks intensify. Unlike hard infrastructure, which may fail catastrophically when overtopped, natural systems adjust and regenerate over time, providing a living line of defense that grows stronger with ecological health. This adaptability gives nature-based defenses a unique advantage in addressing the uncertainties of future climate scenarios.

Wetlands and marshes are among the most effective natural defenses. They act as sponges, absorbing excess water during storm events and gradually releasing it, reducing flood impacts on adjacent communities. At the same time, they filter pollutants, improve water quality, and provide critical habitats for biodiversity. Restoring degraded wetlands near urban waterfronts not only enhances resilience but also contributes to ecological recovery and recreational opportunities. In many cities, once-industrial waterfronts are being reimagined as wetland parks that combine flood management with public access and ecological education.

Mangroves and coastal forests offer another powerful line of defense, particularly in tropical and subtropical regions. Their dense root systems stabilize shorelines, reduce erosion, and trap sediments, helping land build upward in response to rising seas. Studies have shown that mangroves can significantly reduce wave heights and storm surge impacts, protecting both ecosystems and human settlements. Beyond their protective role, mangroves also sequester large amounts of carbon, making them valuable for climate mitigation as well as adaptation. Incorporating mangrove restoration into waterfront planning exemplifies the multifunctionality of nature-based defenses, addressing both resilience and broader sustainability goals.

Sand dunes and barrier islands similarly serve as buffers against coastal hazards. They absorb wave energy during storms, reducing the force of water reaching inland areas. Protecting and restoring dune systems can be a cost-effective way to enhance resilience, especially when combined with vegetation planting that stabilizes sand and promotes natural regeneration. These systems, while sometimes overlooked in urban settings, play a crucial role in maintaining coastal dynamics and offering natural protection that adapts over time.

Riverfront cities are also experimenting with floodplains and green corridors as nature-based defenses. By reconnecting rivers with their natural floodplains, cities can create areas that safely absorb and store excess water during heavy rainfall events, reducing flood risks downstream. These spaces often double as recreational areas or ecological reserves, further demonstrating the multifunctional benefits of integrating natural systems into urban design. The restoration of riverbanks with vegetation, wetlands, and permeable landscapes creates not just protection but also spaces that enhance urban life.

Nature-based defenses do not operate in isolation but are increasingly integrated with engineered infrastructure in hybrid systems. For example, a seawall might be designed to work in tandem with restored wetlands, reducing the wall's required height and cost while providing ecological benefits. This blending of gray and green infrastructure creates more resilient and cost-effective solutions than either approach alone. Such hybrid strategies also help bridge the gap between traditional engineering practices and the growing demand for ecological approaches, fostering innovation in waterfront design.

The social and cultural dimensions of nature-based defenses are equally important. These systems often restore public access to waterfronts, creating spaces for recreation, education, and cultural expression. They reconnect communities with natural processes that had been obscured by industrial or engineered barriers. In doing so, they foster environmental stewardship and raise public awareness of the importance of ecological health for urban resilience. By linking adaptation with cultural and community benefits, nature-based defenses strengthen both physical and social resilience.

Integrating nature-based defenses into waterfront planning represents a critical step toward creating cities that can live with water rather than resist it. These systems provide adaptive, multifunctional, and sustainable protection while also enhancing biodiversity, improving quality of life, and supporting climate mitigation goals. Their success lies in their ability to evolve alongside changing environmental conditions, offering flexible defenses that grow stronger as ecosystems thrive. For urban waterfronts facing intensifying climate challenges, nature-based defenses are not peripheral options but central strategies for building resilient, inclusive, and sustainable futures.

Long-Term Planning for Uncertainty

Urban waterfronts face an uncertain future shaped by climate change, shifting economies, and evolving social expectations. While models project rising seas, more intense storms, and greater variability in rainfall, the pace and scale of these changes remain uncertain. This uncertainty complicates decision-making for cities, which must balance immediate needs with long-term resilience. Long-term planning for waterfronts, therefore, requires strategies that embrace flexibility, adaptability, and foresight, ensuring that these spaces can remain viable and vibrant under a wide range of future scenarios.

A central challenge in planning for uncertainty is the time horizon of climate change. Sea-level rise and associated impacts will unfold over decades and centuries, outlasting political cycles, financial plans, and even the physical lifespan of many structures. Traditional approaches to planning and infrastructure, which often rely on fixed projections and design standards, are inadequate in the face of such evolving risks. Cities must move toward adaptive planning frameworks that can be adjusted as new information becomes available. This requires building flexibility into both physical infrastructure and governance systems, ensuring the capacity to respond to changing conditions without locking into unsustainable or maladaptive pathways.

Scenario planning has emerged as a key tool in addressing uncertainty. Rather than relying on a single projection of future conditions, cities are increasingly developing multiple scenarios that account for different rates of sea-level rise, storm intensities, and socio-economic changes. By exploring a range of plausible futures, decision-makers can identify strategies that are robust across scenarios, reducing the risk of investing in solutions that may fail under unanticipated conditions. This approach shifts the focus from prediction to preparedness, emphasizing resilience under uncertainty rather than precision in forecasting.

Phased implementation is another critical element of long-term planning. Instead of building large, inflexible defenses upfront, cities are adopting incremental approaches that allow for adjustments over time. For example, a seawall might be constructed to a certain height with the capacity to be raised as conditions worsen. Similarly, land-use policies may designate areas for development in the short term while preserving options for future retreat or transformation. This phased approach minimizes sunk costs, spreads investment over time, and ensures that strategies remain responsive to new data and evolving risks.

Institutional and governance frameworks also play a crucial role in planning for uncertainty. Effective long-term planning requires coordination across multiple levels of government, private stakeholders, and civil society. Policies must encourage continuity beyond electoral cycles, ensuring that resilience strategies are sustained over generations. This often involves establishing dedicated institutions, funding mechanisms, or legal frameworks that lock in long-term commitments to adaptation. Engaging communities in this process is essential, both to ensure legitimacy and to incorporate local knowledge into planning. Transparent decision-making and inclusive participation strengthen public trust and foster shared responsibility for adaptation.

Financial planning is equally important in managing uncertainty. Adaptation measures often require significant investment, yet the costs of inaction are far greater. Innovative financing mechanisms such as resilience bonds, climate funds, or public-private partnerships can help distribute the costs of long-term adaptation. Importantly, financial strategies must also account for equity, ensuring that vulnerable communities are not disproportionately burdened or excluded from protective measures. By aligning investment with long-term resilience goals, cities can create stable financial pathways for adaptation under uncertain conditions.

Cultural and social dimensions of planning are frequently overlooked but are critical for success. Long-term adaptation strategies must align with the values, identities, and aspirations of local communities. For many cities, waterfronts carry deep cultural significance, serving as symbols of heritage and belonging. Adaptation strategies that ignore these dimensions risk resistance or failure. Conversely, approaches that respect cultural identity and enhance quality of life are more likely to endure and succeed over the long term. Embedding cultural considerations into planning strengthens resilience by ensuring that strategies are both technically sound and socially meaningful.

Planning for uncertainty requires embracing change as a constant. Urban waterfronts cannot be designed as static landscapes but as dynamic systems that evolve alongside shifting conditions. By combining adaptive frameworks, scenario planning, phased implementation, and inclusive governance, cities can chart pathways that remain viable even as the future unfolds in unexpected ways. Long-term planning, therefore, is less about eliminating uncertainty than about cultivating the capacity to live with it—ensuring that waterfronts continue to serve as vital, resilient, and inspiring spaces for generations to come.

Chapter 3: Waterfronts and Urban Ecology: Nature-Based Solutions for Resilience

Urban waterfronts are critical ecological frontiers where natural systems and human activity converge. Historically degraded by industrial use and pollution, many are now being restored to enhance both resilience and biodiversity. Nature-based solutions offer an effective way to integrate ecological functions into waterfront planning, turning these spaces into adaptive buffers against climate risks. Wetlands, riparian corridors, and green infrastructure improve water quality, provide habitats, and absorb excess runoff. Beyond ecological benefits, they also enrich public spaces, offering recreation, cultural value, and health benefits. By embedding nature into urban design, waterfronts become engines of ecological resilience and sustainability.

Restoring Ecosystem Functions

Urban waterfronts, once rich in natural habitats, have often been heavily modified by centuries of human activity. Industrialization, dredging, land reclamation, and pollution have degraded ecosystems that previously provided critical services such as water filtration, nutrient cycling, flood mitigation, and habitat provision. As cities adapt to climate change and pursue sustainability, restoring ecosystem functions along waterfronts has become a central priority. By repairing ecological processes, urban areas can strengthen resilience, improve quality of life, and create waterfronts that work with natural systems rather than against them.

Ecosystem functions are the foundation of resilience in waterfront environments. Wetlands filter pollutants and improve water quality, reducing the need for expensive treatment infrastructure. Floodplains absorb excess water during storms, lowering the risk of inundation in adjacent urban districts. Vegetated shorelines stabilize soils, reducing erosion and protecting built infrastructure. These services are often undervalued until they are lost, at which point cities face significant costs for remediation and protection. Restoring these functions is not only an ecological imperative but also an economic one, as it offers cost-effective and adaptive alternatives to hard infrastructure.

The process of restoring ecosystem functions begins with reconnecting natural systems that have been fragmented or buried under development. Rivers that were once channeled into concrete canals can be re-opened to flow more naturally, allowing them to reestablish wetlands and riparian habitats. Shorelines hardened with bulkheads or seawalls can be softened with vegetation, oyster reefs, or sediment replenishment, which reintroduce ecological dynamics. Restoring tidal flows to estuaries and marshes reactivates nutrient cycling and habitat provision, creating conditions for fish, birds, and other wildlife to thrive. These interventions not only recover ecological health but also enhance the resilience of waterfronts to climate impacts.

Waterfront restoration also supports biodiversity, which in turn strengthens ecosystem services. Diverse plant and animal communities perform ecological functions more efficiently and adapt better to disturbances. For instance, oyster reefs filter large volumes of water while also creating habitat for other species. Mangroves and salt marshes provide nurseries for fish while sequestering carbon. Reintroducing biodiversity along waterfronts amplifies these services, creating ecosystems that are both productive and protective. This approach underscores the interconnectedness of ecological restoration and climate adaptation.

Another important aspect of restoring ecosystem functions is addressing pollution and contamination legacies. Many urban waterfronts bear the scars of industrial use, with sediments polluted by heavy metals, chemicals, and waste. Cleaning and remediating these sites is essential for restoring ecological processes and ensuring safe environments for communities. Bioremediation techniques, such as using plants and microorganisms to absorb or break down pollutants, are increasingly being integrated into restoration projects. These approaches repair ecological functions while reducing risks to human health and supporting the return of aquatic life.

Restoration projects also provide opportunities for multifunctional urban design. Ecosystem functions can be integrated into parks, promenades, and public spaces that both serve ecological purposes and enhance urban life. For example, a restored wetland along a waterfront may act as a flood buffer while offering walking trails, educational signage, and opportunities for birdwatching. These projects demonstrate that ecological restoration need not be isolated from urban development but can be woven into it, creating spaces that support both people and nature.

Community involvement plays a vital role in restoring ecosystem functions. Local residents often hold valuable knowledge about historical landscapes and ecological changes, and engaging them in planning and stewardship builds ownership and long-term commitment. Public participation in restoration projects—such as planting vegetation, monitoring wildlife, or maintaining green spaces—helps ensure that interventions are not only technically effective but also socially supported. This collaboration fosters environmental stewardship and strengthens the bond between people and their waterfronts.

Restoring ecosystem functions is ultimately about rebalancing the relationship between cities and the natural systems that sustain them. By investing in ecological health, cities create waterfronts that buffer against climate impacts, provide essential services, and enrich urban life. The recovery of these functions transforms waterfronts from degraded industrial zones into resilient, vibrant landscapes where natural processes and human activities coexist. As climate pressures intensify, restoring ecosystem functions will remain a cornerstone of building sustainable and adaptive waterfronts.

Enhancing Biodiversity in Urban Waterfronts

Urban waterfronts, long dominated by industrial uses and dense human activity, have often suffered from severe ecological degradation. Habitats were fragmented, shorelines hardened, and water quality diminished, leading to significant losses in biodiversity. As cities look toward building resilience and sustainability, enhancing biodiversity has become a core strategy in the transformation of waterfronts. Restoring diverse ecological systems not only supports wildlife but also strengthens ecosystem services such as flood protection, water purification, and carbon sequestration. In this way, biodiversity becomes both an ecological and social asset, central to the long-term success of urban waterfronts.

Biodiversity plays a critical role in maintaining resilient ecosystems. Diverse communities of plants, animals, and microorganisms provide redundancy and adaptability, ensuring that ecological functions continue even in the face of disturbances. For instance, a shoreline planted with a variety of native species is more likely to resist erosion and recover after storms than one dominated by a single species. Similarly, aquatic systems with diverse fish and invertebrate populations are better able to adapt to changing water conditions. This ecological resilience directly benefits urban communities by stabilizing waterfronts and reducing risks from flooding and erosion.

Restoring habitat diversity is one of the most effective ways to enhance biodiversity along urban waterfronts. Many waterfronts have lost the mosaic of habitats—wetlands, mudflats, dunes, mangroves, and riparian forests—that once supported a wide range of species. By reintroducing these habitats, cities can provide essential breeding grounds, migration stopovers, and feeding areas. Oyster reefs, for example, not only filter water and stabilize shorelines but also create habitat for fish, crabs, and birds. Similarly, replanting mangroves or salt marshes invites the return of numerous species while providing natural defenses against storm surges. Each restored habitat adds to the ecological complexity that underpins biodiversity.

Connectivity is another key principle in enhancing biodiversity. Urban development often isolates waterfront ecosystems from one another, creating fragmented habitats that cannot sustain large or healthy populations. By creating ecological corridors—such as greenways, riparian buffers, and linked wetland systems—cities can enable species to move more freely between habitats. This connectivity supports genetic diversity, improves resilience, and allows species to adapt to climate shifts. In waterfront planning, designing spaces that link terrestrial and aquatic environments fosters integrated ecological networks that benefit both biodiversity and urban resilience.

Water quality improvements are also central to supporting biodiversity. Polluted and degraded waters undermine the health of aquatic ecosystems, making it difficult for species to survive or return. Investments in stormwater management, green infrastructure, and pollution remediation directly benefit biodiversity by creating cleaner, healthier environments. For example, rain gardens, bioswales, and permeable pavements reduce runoff and filter pollutants before they reach waterfronts. As water quality improves, fish populations recover, aquatic vegetation flourishes, and food webs are reestablished. This illustrates the tight link between ecological restoration, biodiversity, and human infrastructure.

Urban waterfront biodiversity initiatives also offer significant cultural and social benefits. Visible wildlife—such as birds, fish, and pollinators—connects residents with nature and enriches urban life. Green, biodiverse spaces enhance public health by providing opportunities for recreation, stress relief, and education. They also foster environmental awareness, encouraging stewardship among citizens who witness firsthand the return of nature to their cities. By integrating biodiversity into public spaces, cities create waterfronts that inspire a sense of place and pride, while also contributing to global biodiversity goals.

Challenges remain, particularly in balancing biodiversity goals with development pressures. Waterfronts are often prime real estate, and redevelopment projects may prioritize commercial or residential uses over ecological restoration. Ensuring that biodiversity is not sidelined requires strong governance, clear policies, and public support. By embedding biodiversity goals into planning regulations and design frameworks, cities can safeguard ecological priorities even as redevelopment proceeds.

Enhancing biodiversity in urban waterfronts transforms these spaces from degraded industrial edges into vibrant ecological corridors. By restoring habitats, improving connectivity, and prioritizing water quality, cities can create environments where nature and people thrive together. Biodiversity enriches not only the ecological health of waterfronts but also their cultural, social, and economic vitality. In an era of climate change and urban expansion, fostering biodiversity is indispensable to creating resilient, sustainable, and inspiring waterfronts for the future.

Balancing Recreation and Conservation

Urban waterfronts are increasingly being designed to serve as vibrant public spaces, providing opportunities for recreation, leisure, and community engagement. At the same time, they are critical ecological zones, offering habitats for wildlife, natural buffers against flooding, and essential ecosystem services such as water purification and carbon storage. Balancing these dual roles— supporting human enjoyment while conserving ecological integrity—is one of the central challenges facing contemporary waterfront planning. Achieving this balance requires approaches that integrate ecological restoration with urban design, ensuring that both people and nature can coexist and thrive along the water's edge.

Recreation has become a defining function of many post-industrial waterfronts. Where docks and warehouses once dominated, cities have built promenades, bike paths, parks, and cultural attractions. These spaces attract residents and tourists alike, revitalizing urban life and generating economic benefits through increased foot traffic, hospitality, and cultural events. The appeal of waterfront recreation lies not only in its aesthetic qualities but also in the sense of openness and connection to nature that water provides. By offering spaces for walking, cycling, fishing, kayaking, or simply relaxing, waterfronts play a vital role in improving urban quality of life.

Yet, recreational development can come at a cost to ecological systems. Expansive boardwalks, artificial beaches, and high levels of human activity often disturb wildlife, disrupt habitats, and contribute to erosion or pollution. In heavily used areas, the ecological functions of wetlands, marshes, or riparian zones may be compromised by trampling, litter, or noise. The very popularity of recreational waterfronts can place stress on the ecosystems that make them attractive in the first place. This creates a tension: how can cities provide meaningful access to waterfronts while preserving their ecological integrity?

One approach is to integrate conservation goals directly into recreational design. Waterfront parks, for example, can incorporate restored wetlands, vegetated buffers, and natural shorelines that provide habitat while also serving as recreational amenities. Trails can be carefully routed to minimize ecological disturbance, while observation decks and boardwalks can be elevated to allow people to experience sensitive habitats without damaging them. Interpretive signage and educational programs can help visitors understand and appreciate the ecological value of the waterfront, fostering stewardship alongside recreation. In this way, recreational use becomes a tool for promoting, rather than undermining, conservation.

Zoning and spatial planning are also essential in achieving balance. Not every part of a waterfront needs to serve all purposes; some areas can be designated primarily for recreation, while others are protected for conservation. By mapping ecological hotspots and biodiversity corridors, cities can prioritize sensitive areas for restricted access or ecological restoration. At the same time, less-sensitive zones can be designed for intensive recreational use. This spatial differentiation allows for a balance across the entire waterfront rather than forcing each site to meet all demands simultaneously.

Technology and design innovation further support the integration of recreation and conservation. Green infrastructure solutions—such as permeable pavements, rain gardens, and living shorelines—manage stormwater and reduce pollution while enhancing the recreational quality of public spaces. Floating wetlands can improve water quality while doubling as educational features. Lighting design can minimize disruption to nocturnal wildlife while still providing safe access for visitors. These examples demonstrate how careful design can align ecological and recreational functions rather than setting them in opposition.

Community engagement plays a critical role in balancing recreation and conservation. Local residents often have strong connections to waterfronts, whether for cultural, historical, or recreational reasons. Involving communities in planning ensures that recreational spaces reflect local needs while also building support for conservation initiatives. Volunteer programs for habitat restoration, wildlife monitoring, or park maintenance encourage residents to take ownership of ecological health. This engagement helps foster a culture where recreation is not seen as separate from conservation but as complementary to it.

Equity is another important consideration. Waterfronts that prioritize high-value recreational developments, such as luxury marinas or exclusive promenades, can exclude lower-income residents and create inequities in access. Ensuring that recreational opportunities are inclusive and affordable helps prevent waterfronts from becoming enclaves for the privileged. At the same time, equitable access must be balanced with conservation priorities to avoid overuse of sensitive areas. Policies that prioritize both inclusivity and ecological integrity are essential to ensuring fair and sustainable outcomes.

Balancing recreation and conservation requires ongoing monitoring and adaptive management. Ecological conditions and recreational pressures change over time, and strategies must evolve in response. Cities must track the health of habitats, the movement of species, and the impacts of recreational activity, adjusting management practices as needed. This dynamic approach ensures that waterfronts remain both enjoyable and ecologically robust into the future.

The success of urban waterfronts lies in their ability to serve multiple roles simultaneously. By embracing design approaches that integrate ecological restoration with recreational opportunities, cities can create spaces that support biodiversity, foster community, and enhance resilience. The challenge is not to choose between recreation and conservation but to weave them together into multifunctional landscapes. When done well, urban waterfronts can demonstrate how people and nature can coexist productively, creating environments that are lively, inclusive, and ecologically vibrant.

Ecological Connectivity and Urban Networks

Waterfronts are not isolated landscapes but integral parts of larger ecological and urban systems. Their ability to provide resilience, biodiversity, and social value depends on how well they connect with surrounding habitats, green spaces, and infrastructure networks. Ecological connectivity—the capacity of species, energy, water, and nutrients to move freely across landscapes—is essential for sustaining ecological functions. In urban contexts, where development often fragments habitats, restoring and strengthening connectivity along waterfronts is a vital step in building resilient cities. When waterfronts are integrated into broader urban networks, they become corridors that link ecological health with urban sustainability.

Fragmentation is one of the most significant ecological challenges in cities. Development has often severed connections between rivers, wetlands, forests, and coastal ecosystems, isolating habitats and diminishing their ability to support biodiversity. Urban waterfronts, heavily modified by industry, hard infrastructure, and transportation corridors, are particularly prone to fragmentation. Species that once moved freely between terrestrial and aquatic environments often find their pathways blocked by seawalls, roads, or polluted zones. This isolation reduces genetic diversity, weakens resilience to disturbances, and diminishes the ecosystem services available to cities. Addressing this fragmentation requires deliberate efforts to reconnect waterfront ecosystems with the wider landscape.

One strategy for enhancing ecological connectivity is the creation of green and blue corridors. These linear spaces, often along rivers or coastlines, provide continuous habitats that allow species to migrate, feed, and reproduce. In urban areas, such corridors can connect waterfronts to parks, urban forests, and regional ecosystems. For example, a riverfront restored with riparian vegetation may link upstream forests to downstream wetlands, creating a continuous ecological pathway. These corridors not only support biodiversity but also deliver urban benefits such as cooling, air purification, and recreation. In this way, connectivity contributes simultaneously to ecological and human well-being.

Aquatic connectivity is equally important. Many urban rivers and estuaries have been disrupted by dams, culverts, or pollution, preventing the natural flow of species and sediments. Restoring fish passages, removing obsolete dams, and improving water quality are critical steps in reestablishing connectivity between freshwater and marine environments. Such measures enable migratory species, such as salmon or eels, to complete their life cycles while restoring natural sediment dynamics that support healthy deltas and shorelines. These aquatic connections reinforce the resilience of both urban ecosystems and human communities that rely on them.

Urban design and infrastructure planning also have a significant role in ecological connectivity. By integrating green roofs, vegetated streetscapes, and stormwater management systems into the urban fabric, cities can create stepping stones that connect isolated habitats. These distributed green elements provide pathways for pollinators, birds, and small mammals, linking fragmented ecosystems across the city. When connected to waterfronts, they form networks that integrate ecology into the heart of urban systems. This approach recognizes that connectivity is not limited to large-scale corridors but can also be achieved through smaller, strategically placed interventions.

Connectivity is not only ecological but also social. Waterfronts can act as nodes that link people with nature and with each other, fostering stewardship and shared responsibility for ecological health. Trails, boardwalks, and educational spaces along waterfront corridors allow residents to experience ecosystems directly, strengthening cultural connections to water and nature. These social networks reinforce ecological goals, as engaged communities are more likely to support and sustain conservation initiatives. The overlap of ecological and social connectivity creates multifunctional waterfronts that are both environmentally and culturally resilient.

Governance frameworks are crucial in advancing ecological connectivity. Because ecosystems often span municipal boundaries, regional collaboration is necessary to ensure continuity across jurisdictions. Policies that prioritize connectivity in land-use planning, transportation infrastructure, and waterfront development can safeguard ecological functions while guiding sustainable urban growth. Partnerships between government, private actors, and communities ensure that connectivity goals are embedded in decision-making and implementation. Without coordinated governance, local efforts risk being isolated, undermining their broader effectiveness.

Climate change further underscores the importance of connectivity. As species shift their ranges in response to changing temperatures and habitats, connected landscapes become critical pathways for migration and adaptation. Urban waterfronts can serve as stepping stones that help species adjust to shifting ecological zones. By maintaining and expanding connectivity, cities create adaptive capacity not only for ecosystems but also for human communities, which benefit from the resilience and services that healthy, connected environments provide.

Ecological connectivity transforms urban waterfronts from fragmented, isolated spaces into dynamic systems that sustain life, enhance resilience, and enrich urban living. By restoring corridors, reestablishing aquatic flows, integrating green infrastructure, and fostering social and governance connections, cities can create waterfronts that are embedded in larger ecological and urban networks. This holistic integration strengthens both biodiversity and urban resilience, ensuring that waterfronts are not only edges of cities but vital connectors at the heart of sustainable futures.

Chapter 4: Social and Cultural Dimensions of Waterfronts

Waterfronts are not only physical spaces but also social and cultural anchors within cities. They have historically served as places of trade, gathering, and exchange, carrying legacies that continue to shape urban identity today. As industrial uses decline, these spaces are increasingly being reimagined as cultural and recreational hubs where communities connect with water and each other. Festivals, art, heritage preservation, and inclusive public spaces all reinforce the symbolic importance of the water's edge. By embracing equity, accessibility, and cultural diversity, waterfronts can serve as vibrant civic commons that reflect the shared values and evolving identities of urban life.

Waterfronts as Public Spaces

Waterfronts have long held a special place in urban life, serving as gathering points, cultural stages, and areas of exchange. As cities transition from industrial to post-industrial economies, the role of waterfronts has expanded from working landscapes into multifunctional public spaces that reflect changing values around livability, accessibility, and inclusivity. Today, urban residents increasingly view waterfronts not just as edges of the city but as vital commons—places to meet, recreate, and engage with nature. This shift underscores the growing recognition that waterfronts, when designed as public spaces, contribute significantly to social cohesion, cultural identity, and urban resilience.

Public access to waterfronts has become a central theme in redevelopment projects. For much of the industrial era, large portions of waterfronts were fenced off, privatized, or dominated by shipping and manufacturing, leaving residents disconnected from their city's most valuable natural assets. As industries relocated or declined, these areas became opportunities to restore public access. Promenades, boardwalks, and greenways now reconnect citizens with their rivers, lakes, and coastlines, transforming once-restricted zones into shared spaces. This democratization of access repositions the waterfront as a common good, where the benefits of proximity to water are available to all, not just a privileged few.

The design of waterfront public spaces often emphasizes multifunctionality. Parks and plazas along the water serve as spaces for leisure, festivals, and cultural events, while also doubling as ecological buffers or floodable landscapes. Amphitheaters, art installations, and recreational facilities bring vibrancy to waterfronts, making them focal points for city life. At the same time, careful design can integrate green infrastructure such as rain gardens, bioswales, and restored wetlands, ensuring that public spaces also deliver environmental benefits. This multifunctional approach highlights the unique potential of waterfronts to combine recreation, culture, and resilience within a single landscape.

Waterfronts as public spaces also play an important symbolic role. They are stages on which the identity and aspirations of a city are expressed. Signature projects such as parks, promenades, or cultural landmarks along the waterfront often become iconic images that define a city's brand. These spaces embody civic pride, reflecting values of openness, innovation, and sustainability. They can also serve as sites of collective memory, where communities gather to celebrate, protest, or commemorate shared experiences. In this way, the waterfront becomes more than just a physical space—it becomes part of the cultural and emotional fabric of the city.

Equity and inclusivity are critical dimensions of waterfront public spaces. Redevelopment often brings new amenities and higher property values, which can lead to gentrification and exclusion of long-term residents. Ensuring that waterfronts remain accessible to diverse communities requires intentional planning. This can include designing affordable recreational opportunities, providing public transportation connections, and ensuring that cultural programming reflects the diversity of the city. Inclusive waterfronts are those where people of all backgrounds feel welcome, and where public investment is distributed fairly across neighborhoods. By foregrounding equity, cities can prevent waterfronts from becoming enclaves of privilege and instead foster shared spaces that strengthen community bonds.

The role of public participation is equally important in shaping waterfront spaces. When residents are actively involved in the planning and design process, the resulting spaces better reflect local needs and identities. Participatory planning fosters a sense of ownership and stewardship, encouraging communities to care for and sustain these spaces over time. Waterfronts that are co-created with citizens are more likely to succeed as vibrant, well-used public areas, as they embody the values and aspirations of the people they serve.

Waterfronts as public spaces are central to the future of cities. They embody the shift from industrial exclusion to urban inclusion, from private utility to shared amenity. By prioritizing access, multifunctionality, cultural identity, equity, and participation, cities can transform their waterfronts into thriving commons that enrich urban life. These spaces demonstrate how the water's edge can serve not only as a line of defense against climate risks but also as a place of connection, belonging, and collective expression. In doing so, waterfronts fulfill their potential as some of the most dynamic and meaningful public spaces in the urban landscape.

Cultural Heritage and Identity

Urban waterfronts are not only physical landscapes but also cultural and symbolic ones, carrying layers of meaning that reflect the histories, traditions, and identities of the communities that inhabit them. From ancient harbors to modern industrial docks, waterfronts have witnessed the evolution of societies, leaving behind imprints of trade, migration, innovation, and cultural exchange. Preserving and celebrating this heritage is central to the transformation of contemporary waterfronts. As cities reimagine these spaces, attention to cultural identity ensures that redevelopment does not erase history but instead weaves it into the fabric of modern urban life.

Waterfronts have historically been points of first contact between peoples and cultures. They were the gateways through which goods, ideas, and traditions flowed, shaping the cultural diversity of cities. Markets, shipyards, and docks became spaces where different languages were spoken, foods exchanged, and customs shared. This legacy of interaction and hybridity is embedded in the character of many waterfront districts. Preserving this heritage acknowledges the role of waterfronts as cosmopolitan arenas that have always connected local communities to global networks. In many cases, the cultural richness of a city is inseparable from the life of its waterfront.

Built heritage often forms a visible reminder of this history. Warehouses, piers, and industrial buildings, though no longer serving their original functions, stand as monuments to a city's economic and social past. Preserving and adapting these structures allows cities to retain continuity with their heritage while repurposing them for modern needs. Converted into museums, galleries, housing, or cultural centers, such buildings maintain the architectural memory of the waterfront while supporting contemporary urban life. Their preservation also conveys authenticity, ensuring that redevelopment is rooted in place rather than disconnected from its history.

Waterfronts also embody intangible heritage, from fishing traditions and maritime skills to festivals and rituals tied to water. These cultural practices express community identity and continuity, linking present generations to their ancestors. Revitalizing waterfronts provides opportunities to celebrate and sustain these traditions, whether through public events, storytelling, or educational programs. Recognizing intangible heritage ensures that redevelopment projects respect the social and cultural bonds that waterfronts have nurtured over centuries. By embedding cultural practices into the design and programming of public spaces, cities can create waterfronts that honor living traditions as much as physical artifacts.

Identity is closely tied to how communities experience and represent their waterfronts. In many cities, the waterfront is not just another district but a defining feature of local identity. It shapes how residents think of their city and how it is perceived globally. Iconic waterfronts, from the harbors of Sydney to the riverbanks of Paris, have become cultural landmarks that symbolize urban identity. Redevelopment projects that respect and enhance this identity can strengthen civic pride, while those that disregard it risk alienating communities. By embedding cultural narratives into design— through art, architecture, or public interpretation—waterfronts can continue to embody the values and aspirations of the cities they represent.

The integration of cultural heritage into waterfront redevelopment also supports inclusivity. Many waterfronts have histories marked by inequality, colonization, or displacement. Acknowledging these histories openly, through memorials, exhibitions, or storytelling, ensures that redevelopment is not selective in the heritage it highlights. By creating space for multiple narratives, waterfronts can become inclusive landscapes where diverse communities see their histories represented. This approach strengthens social cohesion by validating the experiences of all groups connected to the waterfront.

Waterfronts as carriers of cultural heritage and identity demonstrate that redevelopment is not only about physical transformation but also about meaning. When cultural values are foregrounded, waterfronts become places where history, memory, and identity intersect with modern urban needs. They evolve into landscapes that honor the past while inspiring the future, offering continuity in times of change. By respecting built and intangible heritage, acknowledging multiple narratives, and celebrating cultural identity, cities can ensure that waterfronts remain authentic, meaningful, and deeply rooted in place. This cultural grounding is vital to their resilience, for it ensures that the transformations of today will be embraced and sustained by the communities of tomorrow.

Equity and Access to Waterfronts

Urban waterfronts are among the most desirable spaces in cities, offering aesthetic beauty, recreational opportunities, and cultural significance. Yet access to these spaces has often been uneven, shaped by economic privilege, urban planning decisions, and historical patterns of exclusion. Industrialization, privatization, and gentrification have all contributed to limiting who can live near, use, or enjoy waterfronts. As cities redevelop their waterfronts in the twenty-first century, equity and access have emerged as central concerns. Ensuring that all communities—regardless of income, race, or social status—can benefit from waterfronts is essential for building inclusive, just, and sustainable cities.

Historically, many waterfronts were dominated by industry, ports, and shipping infrastructure that restricted public access. Residents were often cut off from the water by fences, warehouses, and polluted zones. While the decline of industry has created opportunities for redevelopment, new barriers to access have arisen in the form of high-end real estate projects and exclusive recreational developments. Luxury housing, marinas, and commercial complexes frequently dominate redeveloped waterfronts, reserving the benefits of prime locations for the wealthy. In many cases, redevelopment has displaced low-income communities who previously lived in or near these areas, exacerbating patterns of inequality.

The gentrification of waterfronts illustrates the complexity of equity challenges. Redevelopment often raises property values and attracts investment, which can revitalize neglected districts. However, these economic gains frequently come at the expense of affordability and inclusivity. Long-term residents may find themselves priced out of their neighborhoods, while public spaces designed for recreation may cater primarily to tourists or higher-income groups. In such cases, waterfront redevelopment risks reinforcing privilege rather than promoting shared benefits. Addressing this requires policies and design frameworks that deliberately prioritize affordability, accessibility, and inclusion.

Equitable waterfront planning begins with ensuring physical access. Public promenades, parks, and pathways are vital for reconnecting communities with the water. Zoning regulations can require developers to provide continuous public access along waterfronts, preventing privatization of the shoreline. Infrastructure such as public transit connections, bike paths, and pedestrian routes ensures that access is not limited to those with private vehicles or nearby residences. Accessibility must also account for people of all abilities, with universal design features that allow everyone to enjoy the waterfront safely and comfortably.

Economic access is equally important. Recreational facilities, cultural programming, and events must be affordable and inclusive to ensure broad participation. Cities can provide free or low-cost amenities, such as playgrounds, fishing piers, or open-air performance spaces, to ensure that waterfronts serve diverse communities. Policies that support affordable housing near redeveloped waterfronts help prevent displacement and allow low- and middle-income residents to continue benefiting from these spaces. Without such measures, redevelopment risks creating waterfronts that are visually open but socially exclusive.

Community participation is a critical dimension of equity. Waterfront redevelopment projects that fail to include local voices often overlook the needs and aspirations of marginalized groups. Inclusive planning processes, which engage communities through consultations, workshops, and participatory design, help ensure that redevelopment reflects diverse perspectives. When communities have a genuine role in shaping waterfront spaces, they are more likely to feel a sense of ownership and belonging. Participation also helps planners identify cultural and historical values tied to the waterfront, ensuring that redevelopment honors local heritage rather than erasing it.

Environmental justice intersects strongly with equity and access. Vulnerable communities are often the most exposed to flooding, pollution, and other risks along waterfronts. Equitable redevelopment must therefore prioritize resilience measures that protect marginalized groups rather than displacing them. Restored wetlands, floodable parks, and green infrastructure can provide both protection and recreational value, ensuring that resilience is shared. At the same time, equitable planning must avoid creating "climate havens" for the wealthy while leaving vulnerable communities behind. Integrating equity into resilience strategies ensures that all residents benefit from safer, healthier waterfronts.

The symbolic importance of access to waterfronts cannot be understated. Water carries deep cultural, emotional, and spiritual significance for many communities. Denying access to these spaces can reinforce feelings of exclusion and disconnection, while opening them can strengthen identity and belonging. Equitable access transforms waterfronts into shared commons, places where the diversity of the city is represented and celebrated. They become arenas for collective experiences—festivals, markets, recreation—that build social cohesion and civic pride.

Ensuring equity and access to waterfronts is not simply a matter of physical design but of policy, governance, and values. It requires embedding affordability, inclusivity, and justice into every stage of redevelopment, from planning and financing to design and management. By prioritizing equity, cities can transform waterfronts into spaces that embody fairness and belonging rather than privilege and exclusion. In doing so, they ensure that the benefits of living with water are shared across the full spectrum of urban society, creating resilient, inclusive, and truly public waterfronts.

Designing for Inclusive Communities

Urban waterfronts have the potential to become some of the most inclusive and democratic spaces in cities, offering opportunities for recreation, cultural exchange, and social connection. However, without deliberate planning, waterfront redevelopment can easily exclude marginalized groups, prioritize private interests, or reinforce existing inequalities. Designing for inclusive communities means ensuring that waterfronts serve diverse populations, reflect a variety of cultural identities, and promote fairness in access and opportunity.

By embedding inclusivity into the very fabric of waterfront design, cities can create spaces where everyone feels a sense of belonging.

Inclusivity begins with recognizing the diversity of urban populations. Waterfronts must accommodate the needs of people of all ages, abilities, and cultural backgrounds. This involves universal design principles that prioritize accessibility, such as ramps, wide pathways, and tactile paving for people with mobility or visual impairments. Playgrounds, seating areas, and recreational facilities should be designed for multiple age groups, ensuring that children, adults, and seniors all feel welcome. Providing shade, rest areas, and affordable amenities further ensures that waterfronts are usable by all, not just by the young, healthy, or affluent. Accessibility in this sense goes beyond physical design—it creates the conditions for equal participation in waterfront life.

Cultural inclusivity is another essential aspect. Many waterfronts carry deep historical and cultural significance, often tied to indigenous communities, immigrant populations, or working-class traditions. Designing inclusive waterfronts means recognizing and honoring these diverse heritages. Public art, cultural programming, and interpretive signage can highlight the multiple narratives that define a waterfront's identity. Spaces for cultural festivals, markets, and performances allow communities to showcase their traditions and connect with others. By embedding cultural diversity into waterfront design, cities can create spaces that reflect the richness of their populations while fostering mutual understanding and respect.

Social equity must also be considered in how waterfronts are financed and programmed. Exclusive developments such as luxury housing, private marinas, or high-priced recreational facilities risk creating enclaves for the privileged, leaving little room for lower-income residents. To counter this, inclusive waterfronts must incorporate affordable housing, public parks, and free or low-cost amenities. Mixed-use developments that integrate residential, commercial, and cultural spaces at varying price points help maintain diversity and prevent exclusion. Public investment in amenities ensures that waterfronts serve as common goods rather than luxury assets.

Safety and comfort are critical for inclusivity. Public spaces along waterfronts must be designed to feel welcoming and secure for all groups, including women, children, and marginalized communities. Adequate lighting, visible sightlines, and active programming contribute to a sense of safety. Spaces that are well-maintained and actively used discourage exclusionary practices and ensure that no community feels unwelcome. Design elements such as gender-neutral restrooms and clear wayfinding also reinforce inclusivity by addressing the needs of diverse users.

Community engagement is central to designing inclusive waterfronts. Top-down planning approaches often overlook the lived experiences of residents, particularly those from marginalized groups. By involving communities in design processes—through workshops, consultations, and participatory design exercises—cities can create waterfronts that reflect local values and aspirations. Engaged communities are more likely to use, care for, and advocate for waterfront spaces, ensuring their sustainability over the long term. Engagement also fosters trust, signaling that waterfronts are not being designed for an elite few but for the collective urban community.

Inclusivity also extends to resilience planning. Waterfronts face growing risks from flooding and sea-level rise, and vulnerable communities are often the most exposed. Designing for inclusive communities means ensuring that resilience measures protect all residents, not just those living in high-value properties. Floodable parks, green buffers, and emergency infrastructure should be distributed equitably across waterfronts, ensuring that protective measures do not bypass marginalized neighborhoods. Linking resilience with inclusivity strengthens both goals, creating waterfronts that are safe and accessible to all.

The symbolic dimension of inclusivity is equally powerful. When designed inclusively, waterfronts become places where the diversity of the city is visible and celebrated. They serve as stages for civic life, where people from different backgrounds come together in shared experiences of leisure, culture, and community. Such spaces foster social cohesion, reduce segregation, and embody the values of openness and fairness. By contrast, exclusive waterfronts risk deepening divisions, creating spaces that reinforce inequality rather than bridging it.

Designing for inclusive communities is about more than physical access; it is about embedding fairness, equity, and cultural recognition into every aspect of waterfront planning. By prioritizing accessibility, cultural diversity, social equity, safety, participation, and resilience, cities can create waterfronts that truly belong to everyone. Inclusive waterfronts are not only more just but also more vibrant, resilient, and sustainable, as they draw strength from the diversity and creativity of the communities they serve. In doing so, they transform the water's edge into a space where inclusivity is not an aspiration but a lived reality.

Chapter 5: Economic Futures of Waterfronts

Waterfronts have always been engines of economic activity, from early trading hubs to industrial ports that fueled urban growth. Today, as many cities shift toward post-industrial economies, waterfronts are being reimagined as spaces of innovation, sustainability, and diverse economic opportunity. They host emerging sectors such as renewable energy, sustainable tourism, aquaculture, and creative industries, while still supporting global trade and logistics. Redevelopment strategies emphasize balancing investment with inclusivity, ensuring benefits extend beyond private interests. By aligning economic growth with resilience and sustainability, waterfronts can remain vital drivers of prosperity while adapting to the changing demands of twenty-first-century cities.

Waterfronts and Global Trade

Waterfronts have long been at the heart of global trade, serving as gateways for the exchange of goods, ideas, and cultures. From the bustling ports of antiquity to the industrial harbors of the nineteenth century, the prosperity of cities has often been tied directly to their ability to harness the economic opportunities of trade. Even today, as the global economy undergoes profound transformations, waterfronts remain critical nodes in international commerce. Their strategic locations, infrastructure, and connectivity make them essential components of the global trading system, shaping not only local economies but also global supply chains.

The role of waterfronts in global trade has evolved alongside technological innovation. The advent of containerization in the mid-twentieth century revolutionized shipping by standardizing cargo handling, reducing costs, and vastly improving efficiency. Ports that adapted quickly became major hubs of global commerce, while those that lagged behind often fell into decline. This technological shift reshaped the geography of trade, concentrating activity in deep-water ports capable of handling massive container vessels. As a result, some urban waterfronts transformed into highly mechanized logistics landscapes, while others were left with abandoned docks and warehouses as trade moved elsewhere.

Today, waterfronts continue to underpin the movement of goods in an interconnected global economy. Ports handle the vast majority of international trade by volume, making them indispensable to the functioning of supply chains. From electronics and automobiles to food and raw materials, goods flow through waterfronts at scales that directly affect the daily lives of billions of people. Their efficiency and reliability are crucial not only for local economies but also for global stability, as disruptions at key ports can ripple across international markets. Events such as port strikes, natural disasters, or blockages illustrate the vulnerability of global trade to waterfront disruptions, reinforcing their centrality to economic resilience.

Global trade has also introduced new pressures on waterfronts. Larger vessels require deeper harbors and expanded container yards, driving continuous investments in dredging, terminal expansion, and advanced logistics systems. The environmental impacts of these activities, including habitat destruction, air pollution from ships, and carbon emissions, pose significant challenges. Balancing the economic benefits of trade with the environmental costs of port operations has become a critical issue for waterfront cities. In many places, pressure is mounting to adopt cleaner technologies, electrify port operations, and shift toward more sustainable logistics systems.

Waterfronts as trade hubs are also sites of competition and cooperation. Cities and nations invest heavily in port infrastructure to secure positions in global shipping networks. Trade routes shift in response to geopolitical changes, technological innovation, and economic demand, creating winners and losers among waterfronts. Strategic chokepoints such as the Suez Canal or Panama Canal highlight the geopolitical significance of waterfront infrastructure, where control over maritime gateways can shape international power dynamics. At the same time, regional cooperation through port alliances or shared logistics systems demonstrates the collaborative dimensions of global trade.

Urban economies are deeply intertwined with the fortunes of their waterfronts. Ports generate jobs in shipping, logistics, and manufacturing, while also supporting broader service industries such as finance, insurance, and real estate. Yet dependence on global trade can also create vulnerabilities, as cities become exposed to fluctuations in demand, trade disputes, or global crises. The COVID-19 pandemic highlighted the fragility of supply chains and the critical role of ports in sustaining essential flows of goods. These experiences have reinforced the need for adaptive, resilient waterfronts that can withstand global shocks while continuing to facilitate trade.

Waterfronts and global trade remain inseparable in the twenty-first century, but the relationship is being redefined by new challenges and expectations. Ports are no longer judged solely by their efficiency in moving goods but also by their ability to operate sustainably, minimize environmental impacts, and contribute to inclusive urban development. Waterfronts must adapt to the twin pressures of facilitating global commerce and responding to local demands for cleaner air, public access, and ecological restoration. Their future role in global trade will be determined by how effectively they balance these competing pressures, ensuring that they continue to serve as vital gateways to the world while supporting the resilience and sustainability of the cities they anchor.

Tourism and Recreation Economies

As industrial activity has receded from many urban waterfronts, new opportunities have emerged for tourism and recreation to take center stage. Once dominated by shipping yards and warehouses, waterfronts are now being reimagined as vibrant destinations that attract both residents and visitors. Their natural beauty, cultural significance, and central urban locations make them ideal sites for leisure and entertainment. This transformation has positioned waterfronts as key drivers of local and regional economies, generating revenue, creating jobs, and contributing to the identity of cities as attractive places to live and visit.

Tourism is often the most visible dimension of this economic shift. Waterfronts offer a unique combination of natural scenery and cultural heritage that appeals to domestic and international visitors alike. Cities with redeveloped waterfronts often highlight these areas as signature attractions, showcasing promenades, museums, marinas, and cultural venues. Cruise ship terminals bring large numbers of tourists directly to the heart of cities, supporting hospitality industries, restaurants, and retail. Festivals and events staged along the water's edge further draw visitors, reinforcing the waterfront as a cultural and economic hub. This tourism activity not only generates direct revenue but also strengthens a city's global brand and competitiveness.

Recreation plays an equally important role in shaping waterfront economies. Residents benefit from new parks, sports facilities, and open spaces that enhance quality of life and promote well-being. Activities such as jogging, cycling, fishing, kayaking, and sailing bring everyday vibrancy to waterfronts, creating a steady stream of economic activity through equipment rentals, guided tours, and food and beverage services. Restaurants and cafes with waterfront views often become highly sought-after, contributing to the local economy while reinforcing the appeal of the waterfront as a social destination. By serving both residents and tourists, recreational amenities anchor waterfronts as multifunctional urban assets.

The integration of culture into tourism and recreation economies adds further value. Many cities have preserved and repurposed historic docks, warehouses, and piers into museums, galleries, and performance spaces. These cultural institutions attract visitors while also providing platforms for local artists and traditions. Public art installations, amphitheaters, and community markets bring creative energy to waterfronts, blurring the boundaries between culture, recreation, and tourism. In this way, cultural programming enhances the distinctiveness of waterfront economies, ensuring they are not simply generic leisure zones but reflect the unique identity of each city.

However, tourism and recreation economies along waterfronts also face challenges. The popularity of these spaces can create overcrowding, strain infrastructure, and put pressure on local ecosystems. Cruise tourism, for instance, can generate significant revenue but also contributes to pollution and congestion. Over-commercialization may undermine the authenticity of waterfronts, transforming them into spaces that cater primarily to tourists at the expense of local communities. Rising property values driven by tourism demand can displace long-term residents and businesses, raising questions of equity and inclusivity. These tensions highlight the importance of carefully balancing economic opportunity with social and environmental sustainability.

Sustainability is becoming a defining expectation of waterfront tourism and recreation. Visitors and residents alike increasingly value green infrastructure, clean water, and natural landscapes as part of their waterfront experience. Investments in ecological restoration, renewable energy, and sustainable transport enhance the appeal of waterfronts while aligning them with broader climate and resilience goals. Eco-tourism initiatives, such as birdwatching in restored wetlands or educational tours of living shorelines, demonstrate how economic activity can be integrated with conservation. By linking tourism and recreation with sustainability, waterfronts can build economies that are both resilient and responsible.

Tourism and recreation economies are now central to the identity and vitality of urban waterfronts. They provide revenue, create jobs, and enrich cultural life while also strengthening the global image of cities. The challenge lies in ensuring that these economies remain inclusive, sustainable, and reflective of local identity. When managed thoughtfully, waterfronts can serve as dynamic destinations that bring together residents and visitors, culture and ecology, leisure and resilience. In doing so, they transform the water's edge into a shared stage for economic vitality and community life.

Housing and Real Estate Pressures

Urban waterfronts have become some of the most sought-after locations for real estate development. Their scenic views, cultural significance, and central urban positions make them highly attractive for housing, commercial projects, and mixed-use developments. This desirability has intensified real estate pressures, reshaping the social and economic character of waterfront districts. While redevelopment brings investment and revitalization, it also raises questions about affordability, displacement, and the equitable distribution of benefits. Addressing housing and real estate pressures is therefore central to ensuring that waterfronts remain inclusive and sustainable spaces rather than enclaves of privilege.

The appeal of waterfront living is universal. Properties with access to water views or proximity to recreational and cultural amenities command premium prices in housing markets worldwide. Developers capitalize on this demand, building luxury apartments, condominiums, and office complexes along revitalized waterfronts. These projects often redefine skylines and generate substantial tax revenues for cities, reinforcing the perception of waterfronts as engines of economic growth. However, the focus on high-value development frequently limits opportunities for affordable housing, creating waterfronts that serve only a narrow segment of the population.

Gentrification is one of the most prominent outcomes of real estate pressures on waterfronts. As investment flows into formerly neglected districts, property values rise rapidly, often pushing out long-term, lower-income residents. The cultural and social diversity that once characterized waterfront neighborhoods can be eroded, replaced by more homogeneous, affluent populations. In some cases, even cultural or artistic communities that helped spark waterfront revitalization are displaced by escalating costs. This dynamic undermines inclusivity, transforming the waterfront into an exclusive commodity rather than a shared public asset.

The real estate pressures extend beyond housing into commercial and recreational uses. High-value retail, entertainment, and tourism-focused developments often dominate waterfronts, further driving up costs and prioritizing visitors over residents. While these projects can boost local economies, they risk creating spaces that are disconnected from the daily lives of surrounding communities. In extreme cases, redeveloped waterfronts become "islands of prosperity," visually impressive but socially detached from the broader urban fabric.

Cities face the challenge of balancing private investment with public interest. On one hand, real estate development provides critical funding for infrastructure, public spaces, and cultural facilities. On the other, unchecked development risks eroding affordability, access, and ecological integrity. Policies and planning tools are therefore essential in mediating these pressures. Inclusionary zoning, affordable housing mandates, and public land trusts are examples of mechanisms that can ensure a portion of new housing remains accessible to lower- and middle-income residents. Similarly, public-private partnerships can be structured to include community benefits agreements that guarantee investment in local services, jobs, and amenities.

Waterfront housing pressures are further complicated by climate risks. Rising sea levels, flooding, and storm surges threaten the very properties that attract premium prices. In some cities, luxury developments are being built in zones that face increasing climate vulnerability, raising concerns about long-term safety and sustainability. This paradox highlights the need to integrate resilience into real estate planning. Housing and commercial projects along waterfronts must be designed with adaptive infrastructure, elevated foundations, and nature-based defenses to ensure their long-term viability. Without such measures, real estate investments risk becoming stranded assets, with communities bearing the social and economic consequences.

Equity considerations are central to addressing housing and real estate pressures. Inclusive planning must ensure that waterfront redevelopment does not come at the expense of vulnerable populations. Affordable housing, accessible public spaces, and protections against displacement are necessary to preserve social diversity. Transparency and community participation in decision-making processes help build trust and ensure that development reflects local needs. Cities that successfully balance real estate pressures with inclusivity create waterfronts that are both vibrant and equitable, avoiding the pitfalls of exclusivity and gentrification.

Housing and real estate pressures will remain defining forces in the future of urban waterfronts. Their desirability ensures continued competition for land, investment, and development opportunities. The task for cities is not to resist this demand but to channel it toward outcomes that align with broader social, environmental, and resilience goals. By embedding affordability, equity, and sustainability into waterfront development, cities can transform real estate pressures into opportunities for inclusive growth. Waterfronts can then serve as dynamic, shared spaces that reflect both economic vitality and social fairness, ensuring their long-term role as anchors of resilient urban futures.

Sustainable Blue Economy Opportunities

Urban waterfronts are uniquely positioned to play a pivotal role in the development of the sustainable blue economy. As cities transition toward more resilient and environmentally responsible futures, the water's edge offers opportunities to link economic growth with ecological stewardship. The blue economy encompasses activities that use ocean, river, and lake resources for economic benefit while ensuring the long-term health of ecosystems. For waterfronts, this means reimagining traditional industries, promoting innovation in emerging sectors, and aligning development with sustainability goals. Done thoughtfully, these opportunities can transform waterfronts into hubs of green growth, climate resilience, and social inclusion.

A key area of opportunity lies in renewable energy. Waterfronts provide space and connectivity for technologies such as offshore wind, tidal, and wave energy. Ports and harbors can serve as staging grounds for the construction, maintenance, and integration of renewable energy infrastructure. At the same time, urban waterfronts can incorporate localized energy systems, such as floating solar arrays or hydropower from tidal flows, to supply clean electricity to nearby districts. These initiatives not only reduce dependence on fossil fuels but also create jobs and foster innovation in the clean energy sector. By leveraging their strategic locations, waterfronts can position themselves at the forefront of the global energy transition.

Aquaculture is another important dimension of the blue economy. Sustainable fish farming and shellfish cultivation can provide food security, livelihoods, and ecological benefits when managed responsibly. Oyster and mussel farms, for example, can improve water quality by filtering pollutants, while also supporting local economies. Urban waterfronts offer opportunities to integrate aquaculture into multifunctional landscapes, combining food production with ecological restoration and recreation. However, success depends on careful regulation to avoid the environmental degradation that has sometimes accompanied intensive aquaculture practices. By adopting best practices and innovative technologies, cities can develop aquaculture systems that contribute to both economic vitality and ecological health.

The circular economy provides additional pathways for sustainable development along waterfronts. Water recycling, waste-to-energy initiatives, and the recovery of nutrients from wastewater can all be implemented in waterfront districts. Ports and industrial zones located along the water's edge are particularly well-suited for piloting circular economy projects that reduce resource consumption and emissions. For example, waterfront wastewater treatment plants can be designed to recover energy, clean water, and valuable byproducts such as phosphorus. These innovations illustrate how waterfronts can act as laboratories for advancing the integration of circular systems into urban economies.

Tourism and recreation also play significant roles in the sustainable blue economy. Eco-tourism initiatives, such as kayaking through restored wetlands or guided tours of living shorelines, generate revenue while promoting conservation and education. Waterfront cultural programming, such as heritage festivals or maritime museums, attracts visitors while reinforcing local identity. The emphasis on sustainability distinguishes these opportunities from mass tourism, which can strain ecosystems. By linking economic activity with stewardship, sustainable tourism strengthens the role of waterfronts as spaces where culture, ecology, and commerce converge.

Ports, as central features of many waterfronts, are also being reimagined within the blue economy framework. Traditionally associated with pollution and carbon-intensive activity, ports are now exploring strategies to reduce emissions, electrify operations, and adopt cleaner fuels such as green hydrogen. The concept of "green ports" or "eco-ports" reflects the growing recognition that trade and logistics must align with climate goals. By implementing sustainable practices, ports can reduce their environmental footprint while maintaining their role as engines of global commerce. Their transformation highlights the capacity of waterfronts to reconcile economic growth with ecological responsibility.

Social inclusion is a critical component of sustainable blue economy opportunities. Waterfront redevelopment projects often attract significant investment, but without equitable planning they risk excluding vulnerable communities. Embedding workforce training, job creation, and local ownership into blue economy initiatives ensures that benefits are widely shared. For example, renewable energy or aquaculture projects can provide employment for coastal communities while promoting skills development in emerging industries. Inclusive governance frameworks that incorporate community voices help ensure that waterfront economies are not only sustainable but also just and equitable.

Waterfronts embody the potential of the sustainable blue economy to integrate growth, resilience, and equity. By investing in renewable energy, sustainable aquaculture, circular systems, eco-tourism, and green ports, cities can unlock economic opportunities that align with climate and sustainability goals. The success of these initiatives depends on strong governance, technological innovation, and inclusive policies that balance economic ambition with ecological and social priorities. When managed effectively, the sustainable blue economy transforms waterfronts from industrial relics into dynamic, future-oriented landscapes. They become engines of sustainable prosperity, capable of delivering both economic vitality and ecological health for generations to come.

Chapter 6: Governance and Policy Frameworks for Resilient Waterfronts

Governance and policy play a decisive role in shaping the resilience and inclusivity of urban waterfronts. These spaces are influenced by overlapping jurisdictions, diverse stakeholders, and competing land uses, requiring clear frameworks to balance development, ecological health, and public access. Effective governance integrates municipal planning with regional, national, and international policies, ensuring coherence across scales. Policy instruments such as zoning laws, environmental regulations, and public trust doctrines safeguard waterfronts while guiding sustainable development. Transparent governance and participatory approaches further strengthen legitimacy, ensuring communities have a voice. Strong governance and policy frameworks are essential for resilient waterfront futures.

Institutional Roles in Waterfront Management

Effective waterfront management requires the coordinated efforts of multiple institutions that shape how these dynamic spaces are used, protected, and developed. Waterfronts are complex zones where environmental processes, economic activities, cultural values, and social needs intersect. This complexity means that no single institution can govern them in isolation. Instead, municipal governments, regional and national authorities, international organizations, private actors, and civil society groups all play critical roles in shaping outcomes. Understanding these institutional roles is essential for building resilient and inclusive waterfronts that balance diverse interests while responding to future challenges.

Municipal governments are often the primary actors in waterfront management, as they are closest to the communities and urban systems directly affected. City governments typically oversee land-use planning, zoning regulations, and public access provisions, which determine how waterfronts are developed and experienced by residents. They are responsible for integrating waterfronts into broader urban strategies, ensuring that redevelopment projects align with goals such as resilience, equity, and sustainability. Municipal agencies may also manage public spaces, maintain infrastructure, and coordinate cultural programming, making them central to day-to-day governance of the waterfront.

Regional and national governments also play significant roles, particularly in setting policy frameworks, funding large-scale infrastructure, and regulating environmental standards. Coastal protection, flood management, and port operations often fall under national jurisdiction, reflecting their importance to economic security and disaster preparedness. National governments may provide funding for major adaptation projects such as seawalls, storm surge barriers, or large-scale ecological restoration. They also establish environmental regulations that protect water quality, manage fisheries, and guide land reclamation. These broader frameworks shape the context within which municipal governments operate, ensuring coherence across regions and sectors.

International organizations increasingly influence waterfront management, particularly through frameworks related to climate change, biodiversity, and sustainable development. Agreements such as the Paris Climate Accord and the Sustainable Development Goals (SDGs) set global priorities that inform local strategies. Funding mechanisms from institutions such as the Green Climate Fund or development banks provide resources for resilience projects in vulnerable waterfront cities. International collaboration also enables the sharing of best practices and knowledge, helping cities learn from one another's successes and failures. In this sense, waterfronts are not just local concerns but also global arenas of cooperation and governance.

Private sector actors are deeply involved in waterfront management, particularly through real estate development, port operations, and infrastructure investment. Developers play a major role in shaping the physical and economic character of waterfronts, while port authorities and logistics companies influence trade and industrial uses. Private investors often bring critical funding and expertise to large-scale projects, but their involvement also raises concerns about privatization, gentrification, and exclusion. Ensuring that private sector roles align with public interest requires robust regulatory frameworks and transparent governance processes. Mechanisms such as community benefits agreements or inclusionary zoning can help balance profit motives with social and ecological goals.

Civil society organizations and community groups provide another essential dimension to waterfront management. Non-governmental organizations (NGOs), environmental groups, and neighborhood associations advocate for public access, ecological restoration, and social equity. They often act as watchdogs, holding governments and private actors accountable for their commitments. Community groups also bring local knowledge and values into decision-making, ensuring that waterfront management reflects cultural heritage and community identity. Their involvement enhances legitimacy, fosters stewardship, and builds resilience by embedding waterfronts within social networks of care and responsibility.

Collaboration across these institutional roles is crucial. Because waterfront challenges—such as sea-level rise, flooding, and economic transition—cut across jurisdictions and sectors, siloed governance is ineffective. Successful waterfront management requires mechanisms that facilitate coordination among municipal, national, international, private, and civil society actors. Multi-stakeholder platforms, participatory planning processes, and cross-sectoral partnerships are examples of governance innovations that can align diverse interests. These approaches not only improve efficiency but also strengthen resilience by ensuring that waterfronts are managed holistically.

Institutional roles in waterfront management are diverse, overlapping, and interdependent. Municipal governments anchor local governance, national authorities provide frameworks and funding, international organizations set global agendas, private actors drive investment, and civil society ensures accountability and inclusion. The effectiveness of waterfront management depends on how well these institutions collaborate to balance competing demands while advancing long-term resilience and equity. By recognizing and strengthening these roles, cities can create waterfronts that are not only economically vibrant but also environmentally sustainable and socially inclusive.

Multi-Level Governance Approaches

Waterfronts sit at the intersection of multiple scales of authority, from local municipalities to regional, national, and even international institutions. Their management involves diverse issues—urban planning, trade, environmental protection, flood defense, and cultural preservation—that cannot be addressed by a single level of governance. Multi-level governance approaches have therefore emerged as essential for coordinating the responsibilities, resources, and policies of different actors. By fostering collaboration across jurisdictions and sectors, these approaches provide the foundation for managing waterfronts as integrated, adaptive systems that serve both local communities and broader societal needs.

At the municipal level, governance is closest to the day-to-day realities of waterfronts. City governments are responsible for land-use decisions, zoning, and the design of public spaces. They oversee the redevelopment of industrial sites, manage recreational amenities, and regulate development along the water's edge. Municipal authorities also coordinate community engagement, ensuring that residents have a voice in shaping waterfront transformations. Their proximity to citizens makes them crucial actors in balancing economic development with inclusivity and access. However, their authority is often limited by financial constraints or overlapping jurisdictional boundaries.

Regional governance bodies play an important role in managing issues that cross municipal borders. Watersheds, coastal ecosystems, and transportation networks rarely align neatly with city boundaries, requiring coordination at a broader scale. Regional planning authorities can integrate waterfront strategies into land-use, transportation, and environmental policies that span multiple municipalities. For instance, regional bodies may coordinate flood management systems, public transit connections to waterfronts, or ecological corridors along rivers and coastlines. This scale of governance ensures that waterfront management addresses interconnected challenges that extend beyond the limits of individual cities.

National governments provide overarching frameworks that guide waterfront governance. They often regulate coastal and inland waterway management, environmental protection, shipping, and port operations. National agencies fund large-scale infrastructure such as levees, seawalls, or storm surge barriers, which exceed the capacity of local governments. They also set policies for climate adaptation, disaster preparedness, and housing, shaping the conditions under which local governments redevelop their waterfronts. In many countries, national legal frameworks define property rights, environmental standards, and public access requirements that directly affect waterfront use. This top-down influence can either empower or constrain local actors, depending on how policies are aligned with local priorities.

International governance adds yet another layer. Global agreements on climate change, biodiversity, and sustainable development directly influence how waterfronts are planned and managed. Institutions such as the United Nations, the World Bank, or the Green Climate Fund provide funding, knowledge, and frameworks that guide local adaptation and resilience projects. International maritime conventions regulate shipping and trade, ensuring that port operations align with global standards for safety and sustainability. Cross-border cooperation is particularly vital for shared waterways and coastal regions, where ecological and economic systems extend across national boundaries.

Multi-level governance approaches highlight the importance of coordination among these scales. Without alignment, policies may conflict—for example, a national emphasis on industrial port development could undermine local goals of public access or ecological restoration. Conversely, effective coordination allows policies to reinforce one another, creating synergies between local innovation, regional integration, national frameworks, and global commitments. Mechanisms such as intergovernmental councils, joint planning authorities, or participatory governance platforms provide structures for collaboration across scales.

Community participation is also integral to multi-level governance. Local voices must be integrated into decision-making processes at every scale, ensuring that waterfronts reflect the needs of those who live and work near them. Civil society organizations often act as bridges between scales of governance, translating local concerns into regional or national policy discussions while also helping communities understand broader frameworks. By embedding participation into multi-level governance, cities ensure both legitimacy and accountability.

The complexity of waterfronts demands governance approaches that transcend traditional boundaries. Municipalities, regions, nations, and international institutions all bring unique responsibilities and capacities, but their effectiveness depends on coordination and integration. Multi-level governance provides the framework for aligning these roles, balancing local priorities with national and global imperatives. When well implemented, it enables waterfronts to become models of adaptive, inclusive, and sustainable governance, capable of meeting the challenges of climate change, urbanization, and global trade while serving as vibrant, accessible spaces for communities.

Legal and Regulatory Instruments

Legal and regulatory instruments form the backbone of waterfront management, providing the rules and frameworks that guide how these complex spaces are developed, used, and protected. Because waterfronts encompass multiple and sometimes competing interests—economic, environmental, social, and cultural—laws and regulations are essential for ensuring balance. They define property rights, establish environmental protections, regulate development, and determine public access. In doing so, they set the conditions under which waterfronts evolve, influencing whether they become inclusive, resilient, and sustainable or exclusive, vulnerable, and degraded.

A primary legal concern in waterfront management is the issue of property rights. Determining ownership and access to the water's edge can be highly complex, involving overlapping claims from private landowners, municipalities, national governments, and indigenous or traditional communities. Clear legal definitions are necessary to avoid conflicts and ensure fair outcomes. In many jurisdictions, laws establish public trust doctrines that guarantee public rights to navigable waters and shorelines, limiting privatization and safeguarding access. Where these doctrines are weak or absent, waterfronts risk becoming enclosed by private developments, excluding communities from shared resources. Strong legal protections for public access are therefore fundamental to equitable waterfront governance.

Zoning and land-use regulations are also critical tools. Municipalities use zoning laws to determine which activities can occur along waterfronts, balancing residential, commercial, industrial, and recreational uses. In many cities, special waterfront zoning districts are created to regulate development intensity, mandate public access, or require setbacks to protect against flooding. These regulations ensure that waterfront redevelopment aligns with broader urban goals, such as resilience, affordability, or cultural preservation. By shaping the physical form and function of waterfronts, zoning laws play a decisive role in determining their inclusivity and sustainability.

Environmental regulations form another cornerstone of waterfront governance. National and regional governments often set standards for water quality, habitat protection, and pollution control. Laws may require environmental impact assessments (EIAs) for any major waterfront development, ensuring that ecological risks are considered before projects proceed. Regulations protecting wetlands, mangroves, or other critical habitats directly influence what can be built and where. Increasingly, climate adaptation laws require developers to account for sea-level rise and flood risks in project designs, embedding resilience into the regulatory framework. These environmental instruments are essential for preventing ecological degradation and ensuring that waterfronts contribute to long-term sustainability.

Building codes and safety regulations also shape waterfront development. Because waterfronts are exposed to unique risks from flooding, erosion, and storms, laws often mandate specific design standards, such as elevated foundations, flood-proof materials, or setbacks from vulnerable zones. These requirements protect both human lives and property, reducing the long-term costs of disasters. In some jurisdictions, codes are evolving to incorporate nature-based solutions, requiring the integration of green infrastructure alongside traditional engineering. Such innovations illustrate how regulatory frameworks can adapt to new understandings of resilience.

Heritage and cultural protection laws further influence waterfronts. Historic docks, warehouses, and shipyards are often protected under cultural preservation statutes, limiting redevelopment options but also safeguarding collective memory and identity. Legal frameworks may also protect intangible heritage, such as fishing rights or indigenous practices tied to water. By embedding cultural considerations into law, cities can ensure that redevelopment respects historical continuity and community identity rather than erasing it in pursuit of economic gain.

International legal frameworks also play a role, particularly for waterfronts engaged in global trade. Maritime conventions regulate shipping safety, pollution from vessels, and the management of ballast water to prevent invasive species. Agreements on climate change and biodiversity influence national and local policies, guiding how waterfronts address resilience and ecological restoration. These international instruments highlight the interconnected nature of waterfront governance, where local decisions are shaped by global commitments.

Enforcement is a critical dimension of legal and regulatory instruments. Even the strongest laws are ineffective without mechanisms for monitoring and compliance. Municipal inspectors, environmental agencies, and judicial systems all play roles in ensuring that regulations are implemented. Public transparency and accountability mechanisms, such as open data portals or citizen reporting systems, enhance enforcement by empowering communities to monitor waterfront developments.

Legal and regulatory instruments are powerful tools, but they are not static. They must evolve in response to new challenges such as sea-level rise, shifting economic demands, and growing calls for social equity. Adaptive regulatory frameworks that incorporate flexibility and foresight are better suited to managing the uncertainties of the future. By aligning laws with goals of resilience, inclusivity, and sustainability, cities can ensure that their waterfronts remain shared, protected, and thriving spaces. In this way, legal and regulatory instruments are not merely constraints but enablers of the creative, balanced, and just futures that waterfronts demand.

Collaborative and Participatory Models

Waterfronts are complex landscapes shaped by diverse interests, from developers and governments to residents, environmental groups, and businesses. Because of this complexity, collaborative and participatory governance models have become increasingly important in guiding their redevelopment and management. These models seek to bring stakeholders together in decision-making, ensuring that waterfronts are not just planned from the top down but co-created with those who are most affected. By embedding collaboration and participation into governance, cities can build more inclusive, legitimate, and resilient waterfronts.

Collaboration begins with recognizing that no single actor has the authority or expertise to manage waterfronts alone. Governments provide regulatory frameworks, but developers, port authorities, and community organizations hold vital knowledge, resources, and influence. Collaborative models create structures for these groups to work together, share responsibilities, and align their objectives. This can take the form of multi-stakeholder councils, task forces, or advisory boards that bring diverse voices into the planning process. Such arrangements ensure that decisions reflect multiple perspectives, reducing conflict and building consensus around shared goals.

Participatory approaches go a step further by directly involving citizens in shaping waterfront futures. Public consultations, workshops, and participatory design processes give residents opportunities to contribute their ideas and preferences. This is particularly important in waterfronts, which often carry deep cultural, historical, and emotional significance for communities. By engaging residents, cities not only gather valuable local knowledge but also strengthen a sense of ownership and stewardship. Participation transforms waterfronts from projects imposed upon communities into spaces co-created with them.

Inclusive participation is critical for ensuring equity. Waterfront redevelopment has often been criticized for privileging wealthy investors and tourists while displacing marginalized residents. Collaborative models can counteract these patterns by deliberately incorporating voices from vulnerable groups, such as low-income communities, indigenous peoples, and small-scale businesses. Tools such as community benefits agreements or participatory budgeting can institutionalize equity, ensuring that redevelopment delivers tangible benefits to those who might otherwise be excluded. This makes collaboration not just a governance strategy but also a mechanism for justice.

Collaboration also helps balance competing priorities. Waterfronts must serve economic, ecological, cultural, and social roles simultaneously. Developers may push for high-value real estate projects, while environmental groups advocate for restoration, and residents demand public access. Collaborative platforms provide spaces to negotiate these interests, identify synergies, and find compromises. For instance, a waterfront park may combine ecological restoration with recreational amenities, or a mixed-use district may integrate affordable housing alongside commercial development. By fostering dialogue, collaboration ensures that waterfronts evolve as multifunctional landscapes rather than single-purpose zones.

Transparency and accountability are key features of participatory models. When decision-making occurs behind closed doors, communities often distrust the outcomes, particularly if redevelopment leads to displacement or exclusion. Open processes, where information is shared widely and decisions are explained, build trust and legitimacy. Digital tools such as online consultations, mapping platforms, and open data portals are increasingly used to broaden participation and increase transparency. These innovations make it easier for diverse stakeholders to engage and hold decision-makers accountable.

Collaborative and participatory models also support long-term resilience. Waterfronts face ongoing risks from climate change, requiring adaptive governance that can evolve over time. By embedding collaboration, cities create governance systems that are flexible and capable of responding to new challenges. Communities engaged in stewardship are more likely to support and maintain adaptation measures such as floodable parks, wetlands, or green infrastructure. Participation fosters continuity, ensuring that resilience strategies are not tied only to short-term political cycles but are rooted in long-term community commitment.

Challenges remain in implementing these models. Power imbalances between stakeholders can limit genuine collaboration, with wealthier or more influential actors dominating outcomes. Participation processes may also risk becoming tokenistic if citizen input is solicited but not meaningfully incorporated into decisions. Ensuring that collaboration is authentic requires strong facilitation, clear rules, and a genuine commitment to inclusivity. Resources must also be invested in building capacity so that marginalized groups can engage effectively.

Collaborative and participatory models reframe waterfronts as shared landscapes shaped by many hands. By bringing together governments, developers, civil society, and communities, these models foster inclusivity, legitimacy, and resilience. They move beyond narrow economic or technical visions of waterfronts, recognizing them instead as social and cultural commons. When collaboration is authentic and participation meaningful, waterfronts can become not only spaces of development but also spaces of democracy, where the future of the city is negotiated openly and collectively.

Chapter 7: Design and Planning Innovations: Integrating Nature and Technology

The design of resilient waterfronts increasingly relies on the integration of nature-based solutions with advanced technologies. This dual approach allows cities to address climate risks, ecological health, and urban livability simultaneously. Wetlands, green corridors, and living shorelines restore natural functions, while smart infrastructure, sensors, and digital twins provide the tools to monitor, predict, and adapt to changing conditions. Together, they create multifunctional waterfronts that are both ecologically regenerative and technologically adaptive. By uniting natural systems with innovation, cities can build waterfronts that protect communities, enhance biodiversity, and foster inclusive urban futures in the face of accelerating change.

Adaptive Waterfront Architecture

As cities confront the dual pressures of climate change and urban growth, the architecture of waterfronts is undergoing profound transformation. Traditional models of static, rigid infrastructure are giving way to adaptive approaches that recognize water as a dynamic force requiring flexibility and resilience. Adaptive waterfront architecture seeks to design buildings, landscapes, and infrastructure that can coexist with changing water levels, fluctuating weather patterns, and ecological processes. It is not only a technical response to climate risks but also a cultural shift in how cities imagine their relationship with water.

One central principle of adaptive waterfront architecture is flexibility in design. Instead of creating permanent barriers, architects and planners increasingly favor structures that can accommodate variability and change. Floating buildings, amphibious houses, and stilt-based construction allow communities to live safely in flood-prone zones. Parks and open spaces are designed to flood temporarily during storms, absorbing excess water and protecting adjacent neighborhoods. These flexible approaches transform the waterfront into a landscape that adapts rather than resists, embracing water as part of urban life.

Integration with natural systems is another defining feature. Adaptive architecture often combines built forms with ecological restoration to enhance resilience. Living shorelines, green roofs, and vegetated facades reduce runoff, improve water quality, and provide habitats for wildlife. Waterfront promenades may incorporate wetlands or tidal pools, blending human use with ecological function. By embedding natural processes into architectural design, cities can create multifunctional waterfronts that serve as both protective barriers and vibrant public spaces.

Technological innovation supports these adaptive strategies. Sensors, data analytics, and digital twins allow buildings and infrastructure to respond dynamically to environmental conditions. Smart stormwater systems adjust in real time to rainfall, while modular building designs enable structures to be reconfigured as needs change. Materials science is also advancing adaptive architecture, with permeable pavements, flood-resistant construction materials, and self-healing concrete reducing vulnerability. These innovations highlight how adaptive architecture is not static but continuously evolving in response to new knowledge and conditions.

Cultural and social dimensions are equally important in adaptive waterfront architecture. Design choices must reflect the values, traditions, and needs of local communities, ensuring that adaptation enhances rather than disrupts identity. Waterfront architecture that honors heritage while accommodating change fosters continuity and belonging. Public participation in design processes ensures that adaptive architecture is inclusive, responding to diverse voices and avoiding top-down imposition. By linking resilience with culture, adaptive waterfronts become places where communities feel ownership of both their history and their future.

Economic considerations also drive adaptive design. Traditional hard defenses such as seawalls can be costly to build and maintain, especially as sea levels rise. Adaptive architecture, by contrast, often provides multiple benefits that justify investment. Floodable parks, for example, function as both recreational amenities and protective infrastructure. Floating housing developments address housing demand while reducing vulnerability to flooding. By integrating social, ecological, and economic functions, adaptive architecture creates more cost-effective and sustainable solutions than single-purpose defenses.

Adaptive waterfront architecture also challenges conventional urban boundaries. By designing structures that coexist with water rather than excluding it, cities redefine their relationship to rivers, lakes, and seas. This shift reframes the waterfront not as a line to be defended but as a dynamic zone of interaction. It represents a philosophical move toward living with water, where architecture acknowledges uncertainty and change as inevitable. This perspective is crucial in an era of climate instability, when rigidity is increasingly untenable.

Adaptive waterfront architecture is therefore a cornerstone of resilient urban futures. It brings together flexibility, ecological integration, technological innovation, cultural sensitivity, and economic sustainability to create landscapes that thrive amid uncertainty. By embracing adaptation rather than resistance, cities can transform their waterfronts into dynamic spaces that are safe, inclusive, and inspiring. These adaptive designs ensure that waterfronts remain not only habitable but also central to urban identity and vitality in the face of an unpredictable future.

Urban Design Principles for Resilient Waterfronts

The design of resilient waterfronts requires a comprehensive approach that balances ecological, social, and economic functions while addressing the risks posed by climate change. Resilient waterfronts are not static structures but adaptive landscapes that can respond to rising seas, flooding, and shifting urban needs. Urban design principles for these spaces emphasize integration of nature, multifunctionality, inclusivity, and long-term adaptability, ensuring that waterfronts remain vibrant and protective assets for cities.

One central principle is working with water rather than against it. Traditional approaches to waterfront design often relied on hard infrastructure, such as seawalls or bulkheads, to keep water out. While these methods provide immediate protection, they lack flexibility and can cause ecological harm. Resilient design instead emphasizes strategies that accommodate water, such as floodable parks, wetlands, and permeable landscapes. By allowing water to flow naturally and safely into designated areas, cities reduce risks while enhancing ecological and recreational value. This principle shifts the waterfront from a defensive edge to a dynamic interface with water.

Another principle is multifunctionality. Waterfronts should be designed to serve multiple purposes simultaneously, combining flood protection, ecological restoration, recreation, and cultural expression. A park can also act as a stormwater retention basin; a promenade can double as a protective barrier. This layering of functions ensures that investments in resilience also generate daily benefits for communities, making resilience measures more visible and valuable. Multifunctional design also increases efficiency, maximizing the use of limited urban land while addressing complex challenges.

Integration of nature-based solutions is a cornerstone of resilient waterfront design. Restored wetlands, mangroves, and riparian buffers provide natural defenses against flooding and erosion while supporting biodiversity. These ecological features offer long-term adaptability, as they evolve with changing environmental conditions. Incorporating green infrastructure into urban design also improves air and water quality, reduces heat stress, and enhances the aesthetic qualities of the waterfront. The integration of ecological systems ensures that resilience strategies are sustainable and regenerative rather than purely protective.

Connectivity is another guiding principle. Resilient waterfronts should not function in isolation but as part of broader urban and ecological networks. Green corridors linking waterfronts to urban parks, river systems, and regional ecosystems create continuity for species movement, ecological health, and recreational opportunities. At the same time, transportation connectivity ensures equitable access, allowing diverse communities to reach and enjoy the waterfront. Designing connected waterfronts strengthens both ecological and social resilience, embedding the water's edge into larger networks of sustainability.

Equity and inclusivity are also fundamental. Waterfronts are often sites of gentrification, where redevelopment prioritizes high-value housing and exclusive amenities. Resilient design must instead ensure that all communities benefit from access, safety, and opportunity. Public spaces, affordable housing, and inclusive programming should be integral to waterfront planning. Designing for inclusivity requires participatory processes that involve residents in shaping their waterfronts, ensuring that resilience strategies reflect community needs and values. Equity ensures that resilience is not only physical but also social, reducing vulnerabilities across diverse populations.

Flexibility and adaptability underpin all resilient waterfront design. Because the pace and scale of climate change are uncertain, infrastructure and landscapes must be capable of adjustment over time. Modular construction, phased development, and adaptive land-use policies allow waterfronts to evolve as conditions change. Designating areas for controlled flooding, or planning developments that can be relocated, ensures long-term safety without overcommitting to rigid solutions. Flexibility acknowledges uncertainty while maintaining functionality, positioning waterfronts to thrive amid unpredictable futures.

Finally, resilient waterfront design emphasizes cultural identity and stewardship. Waterfronts carry deep symbolic and historical significance, shaping the identity of cities. Integrating cultural narratives into design—through art, heritage preservation, and programming—strengthens the sense of place and community ownership. This cultural grounding ensures that resilience is not just technical but also meaningful, fostering long-term care and stewardship.

Urban design principles for resilient waterfronts thus combine ecological, social, and cultural dimensions with technical innovation. By working with water, layering functions, integrating nature, strengthening connectivity, ensuring inclusivity, planning for adaptability, and embedding cultural identity, cities can create waterfronts that are both protective and inspiring. These design principles ensure that waterfronts remain at the heart of urban resilience, safeguarding communities while enriching urban life.

Smart Technologies in Waterfront Planning

Waterfronts are increasingly becoming testbeds for smart technologies that enhance resilience, efficiency, and livability. As urban populations grow and climate risks intensify, planners and policymakers are leveraging digital innovations to better manage the dynamic challenges of waterfront zones. These technologies, ranging from sensors and data platforms to artificial intelligence and digital twins, allow for more informed decisions, real-time monitoring, and long-term adaptability. Integrating smart systems into waterfront planning represents a critical step toward creating spaces that are both technologically advanced and environmentally sustainable.

One of the most prominent applications of smart technologies in waterfronts is environmental monitoring. Sensors deployed in rivers, harbors, and coastal areas continuously track water quality, temperature, salinity, and pollution levels. This real-time data provides valuable insights into ecological health, enabling early detection of problems such as algal blooms or contamination events. Similarly, smart buoys and tide gauges monitor wave action, currents, and sea-level rise, offering critical information for flood preparedness and climate adaptation. These monitoring systems allow cities to respond quickly to environmental changes while also building datasets that inform long-term resilience strategies.

Flood management and disaster preparedness are also significantly improved by smart technologies. Predictive modeling powered by artificial intelligence can simulate storm surges, rainfall, and sea-level rise under different climate scenarios. Digital twins—virtual replicas of physical systems—enable planners to test infrastructure designs and management strategies before implementation. For example, cities can simulate how a new seawall or floodable park might perform during extreme weather events. Coupled with sensor data, these tools provide dynamic systems for anticipating risks and deploying resources effectively. Smart warning systems, connected to mobile networks, can alert residents in real time about incoming storms or rising water, reducing vulnerabilities and saving lives.

Infrastructure design and management benefit greatly from smart technologies. Ports and waterfront logistics facilities increasingly use automation, robotics, and the Internet of Things (IoT) to improve efficiency and reduce environmental impact. Smart cranes, autonomous vehicles, and digital scheduling platforms streamline cargo operations while minimizing delays and emissions. At the urban scale, IoT-enabled infrastructure—such as permeable pavements with embedded sensors or stormwater systems with adaptive valves—helps manage runoff and flooding in real time. These smart infrastructures not only enhance resilience but also reduce operational costs and resource use.

Energy management is another key area. Waterfronts, often hosting energy-intensive facilities such as ports or tourist hubs, are turning to smart grids, microgrids, and renewable energy systems integrated with digital monitoring. Smart meters and control systems balance supply and demand, ensuring efficient energy use across waterfront developments. Combined with renewable technologies like tidal power, offshore wind, or floating solar, smart systems create opportunities for waterfronts to become models of sustainable urban energy. By aligning energy efficiency with technological innovation, waterfront planning supports both climate goals and economic growth.

Community engagement is also being redefined through smart technologies. Mobile applications and interactive platforms allow residents to participate in planning processes, report issues, and access real-time information about their waterfronts. For instance, apps can share updates on water quality, recreational opportunities, or flood risks, empowering residents to make informed decisions. Augmented reality and virtual reality tools enable citizens to visualize proposed redevelopment projects, fostering transparency and inclusion in decision-making. These technologies ensure that waterfront planning remains people-centered, reflecting community needs and aspirations.

However, integrating smart technologies into waterfront planning also presents challenges. Issues of data governance, privacy, and equity must be carefully managed to prevent exclusion or misuse. The cost of implementing advanced systems can be high, potentially limiting their use in less affluent cities. Moreover, overreliance on technology without corresponding ecological and social strategies risks creating fragile solutions. Effective waterfront planning requires balancing digital innovation with natural systems, robust governance, and community involvement.

Smart technologies are redefining the future of urban waterfronts by embedding intelligence, adaptability, and inclusivity into their design and management. Through environmental monitoring, predictive modeling, smart infrastructure, energy systems, and digital engagement tools, cities can better anticipate risks and harness opportunities. When implemented thoughtfully, these technologies transform waterfronts into resilient, efficient, and inclusive urban spaces that reflect both the challenges and possibilities of the twenty-first century.

Integrating Waterfronts into Broader Urban Systems

Urban waterfronts cannot be understood in isolation; they are deeply intertwined with the larger systems that shape cities. Their success depends not only on the quality of waterfront-specific design but also on how well they are connected to transportation networks, energy systems, ecological corridors, and social infrastructures. Integrating waterfronts into broader urban systems ensures that they contribute to the resilience, inclusivity, and functionality of cities as a whole. This perspective emphasizes waterfronts not simply as destinations but as vital nodes within interconnected urban fabrics.

Transportation is one of the most critical points of integration. Historically, waterfronts functioned as hubs of mobility, linking cities to regional and global trade. Today, their role has expanded to include connections within cities, supporting pedestrian, cycling, and transit networks. Successful waterfront redevelopment often includes promenades, bike paths, and public transit links that connect the water's edge with adjacent neighborhoods and central districts. In doing so, waterfronts enhance urban mobility, reduce dependence on cars, and create accessible spaces for diverse communities. Well-connected waterfronts are more likely to become integrated parts of daily urban life rather than isolated recreational zones.

Energy and utility systems also shape the integration of waterfronts. Many waterfronts host power plants, pipelines, or wastewater treatment facilities that are essential to city operations. Redevelopment provides opportunities to modernize these utilities, aligning them with sustainability goals. For example, waterfront districts can incorporate renewable energy systems such as tidal power, floating solar, or wind turbines, feeding into citywide grids. Wastewater infrastructure along rivers and coasts can be redesigned to support circular economy practices, recovering resources while protecting water quality. By embedding utility upgrades into waterfront planning, cities ensure that these areas contribute to broader goals of decarbonization and resilience.

Ecological integration is another cornerstone. Waterfronts form critical ecological edges where land and water systems intersect, providing habitats, biodiversity corridors, and ecosystem services.

Integrating waterfronts into larger ecological networks requires restoring wetlands, riparian buffers, and green corridors that connect to parks and urban forests. Such integration strengthens ecological health at the city scale, supporting biodiversity while also providing natural defenses against flooding and erosion. This ecological connectivity enhances the resilience of both the waterfront and the wider city, demonstrating the multifunctionality of nature-based solutions when embedded into urban systems.

Economic systems also depend on the effective integration of waterfronts. Ports and logistics hubs are vital to trade, while cultural districts, tourism economies, and real estate markets benefit from waterfront redevelopment. When coordinated with citywide economic strategies, waterfronts can diversify economies and generate inclusive growth. Mixed-use planning ensures that waterfronts provide housing, jobs, and amenities while supporting broader urban development goals. Conversely, poorly integrated waterfront projects risk becoming isolated enclaves of wealth or consumption that do not contribute to wider economic resilience. Integration into economic systems is therefore key to ensuring shared benefits.

Social and cultural infrastructures provide yet another layer of integration. Waterfronts serve as symbolic and civic spaces where communities gather, celebrate, and connect with their heritage. Linking these spaces to citywide cultural institutions, educational facilities, and community programs deepens their value as public assets. Ensuring that waterfronts are accessible to all residents, regardless of income or background, reinforces their role as civic commons. Integration at the social scale ensures that waterfronts are not exclusive or disconnected but reflect and serve the diversity of the broader city.

Governance frameworks play a decisive role in enabling integration. Waterfronts are often governed by overlapping institutions, from municipal authorities to port agencies and national regulators. Coordinated governance mechanisms are necessary to ensure alignment with citywide strategies in transportation, housing, environment, and culture. Multi-sectoral planning bodies, participatory decision-making processes, and regional collaborations all strengthen the integration of waterfronts into broader systems. Without governance alignment, waterfront projects risk fragmentation, undermining their potential contributions to the urban whole.

Integrating waterfronts into broader urban systems ultimately means embedding them within the flows of people, goods, energy, water, and culture that sustain cities. By aligning waterfront development with transportation networks, utility systems, ecological corridors, economic strategies, and social infrastructures, cities can maximize their potential as multifunctional assets. This systemic approach ensures that waterfronts are not isolated projects but dynamic, connected spaces that strengthen resilience, inclusivity, and sustainability across the entire urban landscape.

Chapter 8: Digital Waterfronts: Smart and Resilient Futures

The digital transformation of cities is reshaping how waterfronts are planned, managed, and experienced. Once defined primarily by physical infrastructure, today's waterfronts increasingly rely on digital systems that provide real-time monitoring, predictive analysis, and adaptive management. Smart sensors, IoT networks, and AI-driven platforms track water levels, energy use, and mobility patterns, enabling proactive responses to risks and opportunities. Digital twins simulate future scenarios, guiding investment and design decisions. These innovations create resilient, efficient, and inclusive spaces that adapt to climate challenges while enhancing urban life. Digital waterfronts embody the convergence of technology, resilience, and sustainability in shaping urban futures.

Smart Infrastructure and Sensors

Waterfronts are dynamic environments where land and water intersect, creating both opportunities and risks for urban development. To manage these complex spaces effectively, cities are increasingly turning to smart infrastructure and sensor technologies. These tools enable real-time monitoring, predictive management, and adaptive design, ensuring that waterfronts are safer, more resilient, and more efficient. By embedding intelligence into infrastructure, cities can transform waterfronts into living systems that respond to changing conditions while enhancing sustainability and livability.

Smart infrastructure in waterfronts refers to physical systems—such as flood defenses, transportation networks, and utilities—equipped with digital technologies that allow them to collect, process, and respond to data. Unlike traditional static infrastructure, smart systems are adaptive and interactive, designed to adjust in response to environmental changes or user needs. This approach is particularly important for waterfronts, where climate change is intensifying risks from flooding, storms, and sea-level rise. Smart infrastructure ensures that these areas remain functional and resilient under increasingly uncertain conditions.

Sensors are at the heart of this transformation. Deployed in rivers, estuaries, and coastal zones, they continuously monitor environmental variables such as water levels, salinity, temperature, wave action, and pollution. These data streams provide critical insights into the health and behavior of waterfront ecosystems. For instance, flood sensors can detect rising waters in real time, triggering automatic responses such as closing floodgates or activating pumps. Water quality sensors help track pollutants, enabling cities to respond quickly to contamination events and protect both ecosystems and public health. By providing continuous feedback, sensors make it possible to manage waterfronts proactively rather than reactively.

Flood management is one of the most important applications of smart infrastructure and sensors. Traditional defenses like seawalls and levees are often designed to withstand specific conditions but may fail when faced with more extreme events. Smart flood systems, by contrast, integrate sensors, predictive models, and automated responses to provide flexible protection. Tide gauges and rainfall sensors feed data into forecasting systems that predict storm surges and inundation levels. These forecasts inform dynamic operations, such as adjusting the height of movable barriers or diverting water into designated floodable zones. This adaptive capacity significantly reduces vulnerability to extreme weather events.

Transportation and mobility in waterfront areas also benefit from smart infrastructure. Sensors embedded in roads, bridges, and transit systems monitor traffic flows, structural integrity, and usage patterns. Real-time data can be used to optimize traffic management, prevent congestion, and ensure safety. Smart lighting and wayfinding systems enhance accessibility for pedestrians and cyclists, while automated monitoring of bridges and piers ensures that infrastructure remains safe and reliable. By improving connectivity and safety, smart infrastructure strengthens the role of waterfronts as active parts of the urban fabric.

Energy and utility systems are another domain where sensors make a difference. Smart grids in waterfront districts integrate renewable energy sources such as offshore wind, tidal power, and floating solar with advanced monitoring and control systems. Sensors track demand and supply in real time, enabling more efficient energy distribution and reducing waste. Wastewater treatment facilities located near waterfronts can also incorporate sensors that optimize processes, ensuring compliance with environmental standards while recovering valuable resources. These systems demonstrate how smart infrastructure can align with broader goals of sustainability and circular economy practices.

Community engagement is enhanced by sensor-based technologies that make data accessible to the public. Online dashboards and mobile apps can share real-time information about water quality, flood risks, or recreational conditions, empowering residents to make informed decisions. Such transparency builds trust and fosters a sense of shared responsibility for waterfront stewardship. By linking smart infrastructure with participatory platforms, cities can ensure that technological innovation serves not only efficiency but also inclusivity.

The integration of smart infrastructure and sensors is redefining the future of urban waterfronts. By enabling real-time monitoring, predictive management, and adaptive responses, these technologies provide the flexibility needed to cope with climate uncertainty and urban growth. At the same time, they enhance ecological health, support economic activity, and improve quality of life. As cities continue to modernize their waterfronts, smart infrastructure and sensors will be indispensable tools in creating spaces that are resilient, sustainable, and responsive to the needs of both people and ecosystems.

Digital Twins for Planning and Management

Digital twins are emerging as transformative tools in the planning and management of urban waterfronts. A digital twin is a virtual model of a physical system that continuously updates through real-time data feeds. For waterfronts, this means creating dynamic simulations of rivers, harbors, coastlines, and the built environments along them, enabling cities to anticipate challenges, test solutions, and optimize performance before implementing changes in the real world. By integrating environmental, infrastructural, and social data, digital twins offer a comprehensive platform for resilient, efficient, and inclusive waterfront management.

The core value of digital twins lies in their ability to replicate complex interactions between natural and human systems. Waterfronts are influenced by tides, currents, storm surges, rainfall, and sediment flows, all of which interact with infrastructure, transportation networks, and land uses. Traditional static models provide only snapshots of these dynamics, while digital twins evolve continuously as new data is incorporated. Sensors tracking water levels, weather conditions, and infrastructure performance feed directly into the model, ensuring that it reflects real-world conditions with high accuracy. This capacity for real-time simulation allows planners to predict and respond proactively to emerging risks.

Flood risk management is one of the most important applications. Digital twins can simulate storm surges and sea-level rise under various climate scenarios, helping planners design adaptive infrastructure and land-use strategies. For example, a digital twin might model how a floodable park or movable barrier would perform during a once-in-a-century storm event. It can also identify vulnerable neighborhoods, allowing cities to prioritize equitable protection. By enabling scenario testing, digital twins reduce uncertainty in decision-making and minimize the risk of investing in solutions that may not perform under future conditions.

Beyond risk management, digital twins enhance day-to-day operational efficiency. Ports and waterfront logistics systems increasingly rely on digital twins to optimize vessel traffic, cargo handling, and energy use. By simulating ship arrivals, loading schedules, and storage capacities, digital twins reduce congestion, cut emissions, and improve safety. In recreational or residential waterfronts, they can track crowd flows, energy consumption, or transportation demand, ensuring that public spaces and infrastructure are managed efficiently. These operational applications highlight how digital twins serve not only as planning tools but also as management systems for ongoing performance.

Environmental restoration and monitoring also benefit from digital twin technology. By modeling ecological systems, such as wetlands, oyster reefs, or mangrove forests, digital twins can simulate how restoration projects will affect biodiversity, water quality, and shoreline protection. This predictive capability ensures that investments in nature-based solutions deliver maximum benefit. Continuous feedback from sensors allows managers to track ecological health and adapt interventions as conditions change. In this way, digital twins bridge the gap between ecological science and urban planning, aligning environmental goals with urban development.

Community engagement is another domain where digital twins add value. Virtual models can be shared with residents through interactive platforms, allowing them to visualize proposed projects or adaptation strategies. Augmented reality and virtual reality interfaces enable citizens to "experience" future scenarios, such as how a promenade might flood during storms or how restored wetlands would look. This visualization fosters transparency, builds trust, and empowers communities to participate in decision-making. By making complex data accessible and relatable, digital twins strengthen participatory planning processes.

Challenges remain in implementing digital twins effectively. Developing and maintaining them requires significant investment, technical expertise, and robust data infrastructure. Data governance and privacy concerns must also be addressed, particularly when models integrate social data such as mobility patterns or demographic information. Additionally, reliance on digital tools must not replace community knowledge or ecological understanding; instead, digital twins should complement these dimensions. Successful use depends on embedding digital twins within broader governance frameworks that emphasize equity, resilience, and inclusivity.

Digital twins are redefining how cities plan and manage their waterfronts. By combining real-time monitoring, predictive modeling, and interactive visualization, they provide an integrated platform for resilience, efficiency, and participation. Whether simulating flood risks, optimizing port operations, guiding ecological restoration, or engaging communities, digital twins allow cities to make informed, adaptive, and forward-looking decisions. As climate pressures and urban demands grow, these technologies will play an increasingly central role in ensuring that waterfronts remain safe, sustainable, and vibrant parts of the urban landscape.

Data-Driven Decision Making

Waterfronts are complex zones where environmental processes, economic activities, and social dynamics intersect. Making effective decisions in these areas requires navigating uncertainty, balancing competing priorities, and anticipating future risks. Data-driven decision making has become an essential approach for cities seeking to manage and redevelop waterfronts in ways that are resilient, inclusive, and sustainable. By leveraging large volumes of data from sensors, satellites, modeling platforms, and community input, decision-makers can ground their strategies in evidence rather than assumptions, improving both accuracy and legitimacy.

One of the central benefits of data-driven approaches is the ability to manage environmental risks more effectively. Waterfronts are especially vulnerable to flooding, sea-level rise, erosion, and pollution, all of which can be monitored and modeled with precision using modern technologies. Sensors deployed along rivers, harbors, and coasts collect continuous data on water levels, wave patterns, salinity, and water quality. Satellite imagery tracks shoreline changes, vegetation cover, and sediment flows. These datasets, when analyzed through advanced analytics and artificial intelligence, allow planners to predict hazards, identify vulnerabilities, and design targeted interventions. Decisions informed by such data reduce the risk of costly failures while improving long-term resilience.

Flood management offers a clear example. Rather than relying on outdated historical records, cities can use real-time data combined with predictive models to simulate storm surges, rainfall events, and future climate scenarios. This allows for adaptive flood defenses, where infrastructure such as levees, floodable parks, or movable barriers can be designed and managed based on expected risks. Data-driven approaches also enable the identification of hotspots where vulnerable communities are most exposed, supporting more equitable distribution of resources and protective measures.

Data also supports the optimization of infrastructure and resource use. Ports and waterfront logistics facilities generate massive amounts of operational data, from vessel movements to cargo handling and energy consumption. Analyzing these datasets enables managers to streamline operations, reduce congestion, and lower emissions. Smart grids in waterfront districts balance renewable energy inputs with local demand, guided by data from meters and control systems. Water and wastewater systems use data to monitor consumption, detect leaks, and optimize treatment processes. These applications illustrate how data-driven decision making improves efficiency while reducing costs and environmental impacts.

Beyond operations, data enhances ecological restoration and sustainability. Digital monitoring of biodiversity, water quality, and habitat conditions provides evidence for designing and evaluating restoration projects. For example, sensors can track the performance of restored wetlands in filtering pollutants or reducing flood risks, while drone imagery can monitor the growth of vegetation. These data inform adaptive management, ensuring that ecological interventions remain effective under changing conditions. By grounding restoration in measurable outcomes, cities can make stronger cases for investment in nature-based solutions.

Community engagement also benefits from data-driven approaches. Open data platforms and visualization tools allow residents to access and interpret information about their waterfronts. Interactive dashboards may display real-time water quality, flood risks, or recreational conditions, empowering communities to make informed choices. Data visualizations, such as maps or digital twins, help residents understand proposed projects and their potential impacts. By making data accessible and transparent, cities build trust and legitimacy in waterfront planning. Moreover, participatory processes can generate valuable data themselves, as residents contribute local knowledge and feedback that enrich formal datasets.

However, the use of data in decision making is not without challenges. Data collection and management require significant investment in infrastructure, technology, and expertise. Incomplete or biased datasets can distort outcomes, particularly if they fail to capture the experiences of marginalized communities. Issues of privacy and governance arise when social or mobility data are integrated into planning models. Ensuring equitable access to data is also critical, as exclusive control by governments or corporations can undermine public trust. To overcome these challenges, cities must establish strong data governance frameworks that prioritize transparency, inclusivity, and ethical use.

Ultimately, data-driven decision making transforms waterfront planning and management from reactive to proactive. It enables cities to anticipate risks, allocate resources efficiently, and design interventions that are both evidence-based and adaptable. By integrating environmental monitoring, operational analytics, ecological data, and community input, decision-makers can build holistic strategies that reflect the complexity of waterfronts. The result is not only greater efficiency and resilience but also stronger legitimacy, as decisions are grounded in transparent evidence. In an era of climate uncertainty and rapid urbanization, data-driven decision making is indispensable for shaping waterfronts that are sustainable, inclusive, and prepared for the future.

Integrating AI and IoT into Waterfront Systems

The future of waterfronts lies in their ability to adapt to rapid urbanization, climate change, and shifting economic priorities. Artificial Intelligence (AI) and the Internet of Things (IoT) are playing a transformative role in this process by embedding intelligence and connectivity into waterfront systems. Together, these technologies enable real-time monitoring, predictive analysis, and automated responses, allowing waterfronts to function as dynamic, resilient, and people-centered spaces. Integrating AI and IoT not only addresses immediate challenges such as flooding and pollution but also unlocks opportunities for innovation, sustainability, and inclusive urban growth.

AI and IoT integration begins with data collection and connectivity. IoT devices—sensors, cameras, drones, and smart meters—gather continuous streams of data on environmental conditions, infrastructure performance, and human activity. Along a waterfront, sensors can monitor water levels, salinity, currents, temperature, and air quality. Smart infrastructure, such as connected pumps, valves, and lighting systems, can respond to these inputs in real time. AI adds a critical layer of intelligence by analyzing this data, identifying patterns, and predicting future conditions. The combination of IoT's ability to sense and AI's ability to interpret transforms raw information into actionable insights.

Flood management is one of the most powerful applications. Traditional static defenses often fall short under extreme climate events, but AI and IoT enable adaptive systems. Networks of water-level sensors and rainfall monitors feed data into AI-driven predictive models that simulate potential flooding scenarios. These models can trigger automated responses, such as activating pumps, opening diversion channels, or temporarily closing vulnerable infrastructure. AI can also prioritize which neighborhoods or assets to protect based on real-time vulnerability assessments. This creates a responsive flood management system that adapts to changing conditions and minimizes damage.

Water quality monitoring is another critical function. IoT sensors deployed in rivers, lakes, and harbors continuously measure pollutants, turbidity, dissolved oxygen, and temperature. AI algorithms analyze these datasets to identify contamination sources, predict harmful algal blooms, and recommend interventions. Automated alerts can notify authorities or even activate treatment systems when thresholds are exceeded. By linking monitoring with intelligent responses, AI and IoT protect both ecosystems and human health while reducing the costs of manual sampling and testing.

Ports and logistics also benefit significantly from these technologies. IoT devices track vessel movements, cargo handling, and energy use, feeding data into AI systems that optimize scheduling and reduce congestion. Predictive analytics can forecast demand, streamline customs processes, and reduce downtime. Automation, informed by AI and IoT, improves efficiency while lowering emissions from idling ships and trucks. These innovations position ports as smart logistics hubs, balancing economic competitiveness with sustainability.

Urban mobility around waterfronts is enhanced through IoT-enabled infrastructure and AI-driven management. Smart traffic sensors and cameras monitor flows of cars, bicycles, and pedestrians, while AI optimizes signal timing or reroutes traffic to reduce congestion. Public transport linked to waterfront districts can be managed dynamically based on demand. Even public spaces benefit: AI-driven lighting systems adjust brightness according to activity and safety needs, reducing energy use while ensuring comfort. This creates waterfronts that are not only functional but also accessible and welcoming.

Community engagement is strengthened by AI and IoT as well. Public-facing platforms can display real-time information about flood risks, air quality, or recreational conditions, empowering residents to make informed choices. Interactive dashboards and mobile apps allow citizens to report issues, access environmental data, or participate in planning processes. AI-driven visualization tools, such as augmented reality models, can show how waterfronts might look under future climate scenarios, improving transparency and trust in planning decisions.

Challenges remain in deploying these technologies. Infrastructure costs, data privacy concerns, and digital divides can limit adoption. Without inclusive policies, there is a risk that the benefits of smart waterfronts will primarily serve wealthier communities while excluding vulnerable groups. AI models can also inherit biases from incomplete or skewed datasets, leading to inequitable outcomes. Addressing these challenges requires strong governance frameworks, equitable investment, and community-centered design principles.

Integrating AI and IoT into waterfront systems is reshaping the relationship between cities and water. By enabling intelligent monitoring, predictive management, and inclusive engagement, these technologies transform waterfronts into adaptive, resilient, and sustainable spaces. From flood protection and water quality to port efficiency and community access, AI and IoT provide the tools needed to navigate uncertainty while enhancing urban life. Their integration marks a critical step in ensuring that waterfronts remain not only economic and ecological assets but also inclusive and vibrant public spaces for the future.

Chapter 9: Envisioning the Future Waterfront: Resilience, Equity, and Sustainability

The waterfronts of the future will be measured not only by their economic value but by their ability to safeguard communities, restore ecosystems, and foster inclusive urban life. As climate change intensifies, resilience becomes a defining imperative, requiring adaptive designs and nature-based solutions. Equity ensures that access, housing, and opportunities along the water's edge are shared broadly, preventing exclusion or displacement. Sustainability demands circular resource use, clean energy, and ecological regeneration. Together, these principles reimagine waterfronts as multifunctional commons—safe, vibrant, and just— where environmental stewardship and social well-being shape the foundation of long-term urban prosperity.

Scenarios for 2050 and Beyond

The future of urban waterfronts will be shaped by converging forces of climate change, technological innovation, demographic shifts, and economic restructuring. By 2050, cities will face heightened risks from sea-level rise, flooding, and storms, but they will also have opportunities to transform their waterfronts into resilient, adaptive, and inclusive spaces. Considering a range of possible futures allows planners and policymakers to prepare for uncertainty while guiding investments and governance toward sustainable outcomes. Several scenarios illustrate different pathways that waterfronts may take in the decades ahead.

One scenario envisions waterfronts as climate adaptation strongholds. In this future, sea-level rise has accelerated beyond earlier projections, placing immense pressure on coastal and riverine cities. Waterfronts become critical defensive zones, redesigned with floodable parks, living shorelines, floating neighborhoods, and protective barriers. Nature-based solutions are mainstream, with wetlands, mangroves, and oyster reefs integrated into urban systems as buffers against storm surges. Adaptive infrastructure, such as amphibious housing and flexible public spaces, reflects a shift toward living with water rather than fighting it. In this scenario, waterfronts embody resilience, functioning as laboratories of climate adaptation and survival.

A second scenario emphasizes the waterfront as an economic and technological frontier. By 2050, the sustainable blue economy has expanded significantly, with waterfronts serving as hubs for renewable energy, aquaculture, and circular economy industries. Ports are transformed into green logistics centers powered by clean energy, while offshore wind, tidal, and floating solar farms generate substantial electricity for urban districts. Smart technologies— including digital twins, AI-driven monitoring, and IoT-enabled infrastructure—govern waterfront operations, ensuring efficiency and sustainability. These zones not only support local economies but also contribute to global climate goals, positioning waterfronts as engines of green growth and innovation.

Another possible future centers on social inclusivity and cultural identity. In this scenario, cities recognize waterfronts as commons that must be accessible to all residents, not just elites. Redevelopment emphasizes equity, ensuring that affordable housing, public parks, and community spaces line the water's edge. Cultural programming, heritage preservation, and public art reinforce identity and inclusivity, making waterfronts stages for civic life and collective memory. Rather than exclusive enclaves of luxury real estate or tourist consumption, waterfronts become democratic spaces where diverse communities connect with water and with each other. Social resilience is as important as physical resilience, ensuring that waterfront benefits are broadly shared.

A more dystopian scenario is also possible. If adaptation and inclusivity are neglected, waterfronts may become zones of exclusion and vulnerability. Rising seas could render large areas uninhabitable, displacing millions of people and creating climate refugees. Redevelopment dominated by private interests may result in enclaves of fortified wealth, where only affluent populations can afford protection. Meanwhile, marginalized communities are left exposed to risks or pushed inland to less desirable areas. In this scenario, waterfronts become symbols of inequality and climate injustice, highlighting the consequences of failing to plan proactively and equitably.

Finally, a hybrid scenario envisions waterfronts as multifunctional nodes in interconnected urban systems. Here, resilience, economic vitality, social inclusion, and cultural identity are woven together into integrated strategies. Waterfronts act as connectors, linking ecological corridors, transit networks, and social infrastructures. They serve as hubs for innovation while also safeguarding heritage and providing equitable public access. By 2050 and beyond, these waterfronts exemplify how cities can balance complexity and uncertainty through adaptive, systemic design.

The future of waterfronts will likely combine elements from all these scenarios, shaped by local conditions and global forces. What is clear is that decisions made today will determine whether waterfronts become sites of vulnerability and exclusion or resilience and opportunity. Scenarios for 2050 and beyond remind us that waterfronts are not just physical landscapes but also reflections of values, choices, and governance. Planning with foresight, inclusivity, and adaptability will be essential to ensure that they remain vital parts of urban life in an uncertain future.

Integrating Circular Economy Principles

Waterfronts are uniquely positioned to showcase the potential of circular economy strategies, given their intersection of natural systems, urban development, and economic activity. Historically, many waterfronts were centers of linear resource flows—ports moving goods globally, factories consuming materials and discharging waste, and cities directing untreated runoff into rivers and seas. Today, as the impacts of resource depletion, pollution, and climate change intensify, there is a growing recognition that waterfronts can instead become hubs of circularity. By reimagining resource use, waste management, and design, waterfronts can shift from extractive systems to regenerative ones that sustain both urban life and ecosystems.

A central principle of the circular economy is designing out waste. Applied to waterfronts, this involves rethinking how buildings, infrastructure, and public spaces are constructed and maintained. Using modular and recyclable materials allows waterfront developments to be adapted or disassembled as conditions change, minimizing construction waste. Adaptive reuse of historic industrial buildings along waterfronts also reflects this principle, as structures are repurposed rather than demolished. By adopting design strategies that anticipate change, waterfronts reduce the environmental footprint of development while honoring their historical legacies.

Waterfront industries can also become key drivers of circular practices. Ports and logistics centers generate significant waste, energy use, and emissions, but circular economy principles provide pathways to reduce these impacts. Closed-loop supply chains, where materials are reused or recycled locally, reduce dependence on virgin resources. Industrial symbiosis—where waste from one activity becomes input for another—can be facilitated in waterfront industrial clusters. For example, excess heat from shipping terminals could be repurposed for district heating, while organic waste from markets could be converted into bioenergy. These synergies reduce resource intensity while stimulating innovation and new business models.

Water and nutrient cycles are particularly relevant in waterfront contexts. Cities often discharge stormwater and wastewater into rivers and seas, carrying pollutants that degrade ecosystems. Circular approaches seek to close these loops by treating and reusing water for irrigation, cooling, or even potable use. Nutrient recovery from wastewater plants along waterfronts can provide fertilizers for urban agriculture or green corridors. Green infrastructure—rain gardens, bioswales, wetlands—captures and filters runoff, reducing pollution while creating habitats. By cycling water and nutrients back into productive systems, waterfronts can address both ecological health and urban sustainability.

Energy is another domain where circularity strengthens waterfront resilience. Renewable energy sources, including tidal, wave, offshore wind, and floating solar, are particularly suited to waterfront locations. These can be integrated into microgrids that optimize local consumption and storage, reducing dependence on centralized fossil fuel systems. Circularity also emphasizes energy efficiency, where smart infrastructure ensures that waterfront lighting, transportation, and port operations minimize waste. Energy recovered from waste streams—such as methane capture from organic matter—adds another layer of circular practice. Together, these strategies make waterfronts both producers and efficient users of clean energy.

Circular economy principles also extend to tourism and recreation, which are central to many redeveloped waterfronts. Instead of resource-intensive models based on mass consumption, waterfronts can promote low-impact, regenerative forms of tourism. Restaurants and entertainment venues can prioritize local sourcing, food waste reduction, and recycling. Events and festivals held along waterfronts can be designed with zero-waste goals, showcasing circular practices to residents and visitors alike. By embedding circularity in cultural and recreational activities, waterfronts become platforms for public education and behavior change.

Social equity is an essential dimension of integrating circular economy principles. Waterfront redevelopment often risks gentrification and exclusion, but circular strategies can create inclusive opportunities. Community-based recycling, urban farming, and renewable energy cooperatives provide jobs and empower local residents. Ensuring that benefits of resource efficiency, clean energy, and reduced pollution reach marginalized communities prevents waterfront circularity from becoming another driver of inequality. Governance structures that embed participation and transparency help ensure that circular economy strategies are inclusive as well as sustainable.

Integrating circular economy principles into waterfronts redefines their role from extractive gateways to regenerative hubs. By designing out waste, closing loops in water and energy systems, and fostering industrial and social synergies, waterfronts can exemplify how circularity contributes to resilience, equity, and ecological health. In doing so, they showcase how cities can align economic activity with environmental responsibility, turning the water's edge into a model of sustainable urban futures.

Designing for Flexibility and Change

Waterfronts are dynamic landscapes shaped by tides, climate, economies, and shifting social priorities. Designing them for flexibility and change has become an essential principle in twenty-first-century urban planning. Rather than treating waterfronts as static zones fixed in time, cities increasingly view them as adaptive interfaces between land and water, capable of accommodating uncertainty and transformation. Flexible design ensures that waterfronts remain resilient to climate risks, responsive to evolving community needs, and relevant to future urban growth.

One key dimension of flexibility is the capacity to adapt to climate change. Rising sea levels, stronger storms, and unpredictable flooding patterns demand infrastructure and landscapes that can adjust over time. Instead of building rigid defenses that may be overwhelmed, cities are experimenting with adaptable strategies such as floodable parks, movable barriers, and amphibious buildings. These designs are intended not as permanent solutions but as systems that can evolve alongside environmental shifts. By embedding adaptability, waterfronts become living infrastructures, prepared to meet uncertain futures.

Temporal flexibility is also vital. Waterfronts serve multiple purposes across different timescales: daily recreational use, seasonal cultural programming, and long-term adaptation to climate or demographic change. Designing spaces that can transition smoothly between functions maximizes value and resilience. Open plazas, for example, can host markets, festivals, or floodwater retention depending on the context. Multi-use designs ensure that no space is single-purpose or underutilized, creating vibrant, resource-efficient waterfronts that can pivot as needs change.

Architectural flexibility reinforces this principle. Buildings along the water's edge are increasingly being designed for modularity, allowing them to be expanded, reconfigured, or even relocated. Mixed-use developments integrate housing, commerce, and cultural spaces within adaptable frameworks, supporting shifts in demand without requiring demolition. This architectural agility reduces waste, lowers costs, and aligns with circular economy principles by designing for reuse and transformation. Waterfronts built with modular and reversible construction are better able to withstand economic cycles and changing land-use priorities.

Flexibility also applies to governance and management. Because waterfronts involve multiple stakeholders—governments, developers, communities, and environmental groups—management systems must be capable of adjusting as new challenges arise. Collaborative and participatory models provide pathways for ongoing adaptation, ensuring that decision-making reflects evolving needs and knowledge. Governance frameworks that embrace experimentation, pilot projects, and iterative learning allow waterfronts to remain responsive over time, rather than locked into outdated plans.

Ecological flexibility is another layer. Healthy ecosystems naturally adapt to fluctuations in water levels, sediment flows, and species migration. Designing waterfronts to restore and support these ecological processes enhances their resilience. Living shorelines, wetlands, and riparian corridors provide habitats while also adjusting dynamically to hydrological changes. These systems not only buffer cities against floods but also evolve as natural conditions shift, embodying the principle of designing with change rather than resisting it.

Cultural and social dimensions further underscore the importance of flexibility. Waterfronts are sites of identity, heritage, and gathering, yet cultural uses shift with time. Designing flexible public spaces allows new generations to reinterpret waterfronts without erasing their historical significance. Art installations, memorials, and cultural venues can be integrated into adaptable spaces that evolve alongside community narratives. This ensures that waterfronts remain meaningful across generations while allowing for diverse and changing cultural expressions.

Technological innovation enhances this adaptability. Smart infrastructure, powered by sensors and AI, allows waterfront systems to monitor conditions in real time and respond dynamically. Lighting, water pumps, and transportation systems can adjust automatically to usage patterns or environmental data. Digital twins provide platforms for simulating future scenarios, enabling planners to test and refine strategies before implementing them. Technology adds agility to waterfront systems, ensuring they can pivot in response to emerging risks or opportunities.

Designing for flexibility and change is ultimately about embracing uncertainty. Waterfronts will never be static; they are constantly reshaped by natural forces, economic transitions, and social priorities. By embedding adaptability into architecture, infrastructure, governance, and culture, cities can ensure that waterfronts remain resilient, inclusive, and vibrant. Flexible design transforms the water's edge into a space of opportunity, where resilience is not achieved by resisting change but by welcoming and harnessing it.

Building Collective Urban Futures

The future of waterfronts is inseparable from the broader question of how cities can foster collective, inclusive, and sustainable urban futures. These landscapes, situated at the dynamic boundary between land and water, embody the opportunities and challenges of contemporary urbanization: climate resilience, economic transformation, cultural identity, and social equity. Designing for collective urban futures means reimagining waterfronts as shared spaces that integrate diverse voices, balance competing demands, and contribute to the resilience of entire cities.

At the heart of this vision is the recognition that waterfronts are public assets. They are not merely real estate to be developed but vital commons that should serve the needs of all citizens. Building collective urban futures requires prioritizing inclusivity in planning and ensuring that waterfronts remain accessible, affordable, and culturally meaningful. Public promenades, open parks, and cultural venues along waterfronts act as democratic spaces where people from all backgrounds can gather, reinforcing the sense of shared belonging. By resisting exclusive privatization, cities can ensure that waterfronts strengthen community bonds rather than deepen divisions.

Collaboration is central to shaping these futures. Because waterfronts involve multiple stakeholders—governments, private developers, port authorities, environmental groups, and local residents—decision-making must move beyond siloed approaches. Multi-stakeholder governance models create platforms for dialogue and shared responsibility, aligning diverse interests with long-term goals. These collaborative processes help avoid conflicts, foster innovation, and ensure that the benefits of redevelopment are distributed fairly. The creation of transparent participatory structures, such as advisory councils or community assemblies, is essential to embedding collective decision-making into waterfront governance.

Sustainability is another foundation of collective urban futures. Waterfronts are increasingly vulnerable to climate risks, and their resilience depends on integrating ecological processes into urban systems. Restoring wetlands, creating living shorelines, and adopting nature-based defenses enhance resilience while delivering co-benefits such as biodiversity, cooling, and recreation. These strategies reflect a collective responsibility to future generations, ensuring that waterfronts remain habitable and healthy. By aligning resilience with inclusivity, cities can create waterfronts that not only withstand environmental challenges but also improve quality of life for all residents.

Technology plays a complementary role in this vision. Smart systems, digital twins, and IoT-enabled infrastructure provide tools for monitoring conditions, simulating scenarios, and engaging communities. When used responsibly, these technologies enhance transparency and inclusivity by making complex information accessible to the public. Interactive models allow citizens to visualize future risks or design proposals, empowering them to participate meaningfully in decision-making. By embedding technology into participatory frameworks, cities can ensure that innovation serves collective rather than exclusive interests.

Cultural identity and heritage are equally important in building collective urban futures. Waterfronts are often deeply tied to the histories and traditions of local communities, serving as sites of memory and cultural exchange. Preserving and celebrating these identities ensures continuity while allowing new generations to reinterpret and shape the waterfront. Public art, storytelling, and cultural programming can reinforce these identities, making waterfronts places where diverse narratives coexist. This cultural grounding strengthens social cohesion and ensures that redevelopment reflects the values of the communities it serves.

Finally, building collective futures requires governance structures that are adaptive and just. Legal and regulatory instruments must safeguard public access, prioritize equity, and embed resilience into land-use planning. Policies that promote affordable housing, inclusive programming, and equitable investment are essential for preventing waterfronts from becoming exclusive enclaves. Transparent monitoring and accountability mechanisms ensure that commitments to inclusivity and sustainability are not rhetorical but realized in practice.

In envisioning waterfronts as collective urban futures, cities affirm the principle that the water's edge belongs to everyone. By embedding inclusivity, collaboration, sustainability, technology, cultural identity, and adaptive governance, waterfronts become more than sites of development—they become platforms for democratic life, resilience, and shared prosperity. In this way, they exemplify the possibility of cities that are not only livable but also equitable and united, capable of thriving together in the face of twenty-first-century challenges.

Conclusion

The future of urban waterfronts reflects the broader challenges and opportunities facing cities in the twenty-first century. Once dominated by industry and trade, these spaces are now being reimagined as multifunctional landscapes that integrate resilience, inclusivity, and sustainability. Throughout this book, the themes of climate adaptation, ecological restoration, social equity, technological innovation, and circular economy principles have revealed the critical role waterfronts play in shaping urban futures. Their transformation is not merely a matter of design or engineering but a reflection of evolving values—how societies balance growth with stewardship, access with exclusivity, and short-term gain with long-term resilience.

Waterfronts are uniquely positioned at the interface of human settlement and natural systems, making them both vulnerable to environmental risks and vital for adaptation. As sea-level rise and flooding intensify, these spaces will increasingly serve as frontlines of climate resilience. Nature-based solutions, adaptive infrastructure, and flexible design strategies demonstrate how cities can live with water rather than resist it. By integrating ecological systems into urban planning, waterfronts can safeguard communities while enhancing biodiversity and cultural identity. This dual role underscores their significance not only as protective buffers but also as regenerative landscapes that contribute to broader ecological health.

Equity and inclusivity emerge as equally vital principles. Without careful planning, waterfront redevelopment risks becoming exclusive enclaves, dominated by luxury housing and commercial interests that displace vulnerable populations. Ensuring access for all requires deliberate policies—affordable housing, public spaces, cultural programming, and participatory governance—that embed justice into every stage of development. When waterfronts are accessible and inclusive, they strengthen civic identity, create shared experiences, and serve as democratic commons where diverse communities can gather and connect.

Technological innovation provides powerful tools for managing complexity and uncertainty. Smart infrastructure, IoT networks, AI-driven models, and digital twins enhance monitoring, predictive planning, and operational efficiency. Yet technology must be embedded within transparent, inclusive governance frameworks that prioritize equity and accountability. When aligned with human and ecological priorities, digital innovations enable cities to anticipate risks, optimize resources, and foster more adaptive and resilient waterfronts.

The transition to circular economy principles further strengthens the sustainability of waterfront systems. By closing loops in water, energy, and materials, and by promoting reuse, resource efficiency, and ecological regeneration, circular strategies transform waterfronts into hubs of innovation and sustainability. This shift redefines them as not just economic gateways but regenerative landscapes that support long-term prosperity while reducing environmental impact.

Ultimately, waterfronts embody the collective choices cities make about their futures. They are mirrors of governance, culture, and identity, revealing whether societies prioritize exclusivity or inclusivity, resistance or adaptation, exploitation or regeneration. By adopting holistic approaches that integrate climate resilience, social equity, ecological health, technological innovation, and circularity, cities can ensure their waterfronts remain vibrant, adaptive, and meaningful in the face of uncertainty.

The waterfronts of the future will not be static spaces but evolving commons where resilience is lived, diversity is celebrated, and sustainability is practiced. In building them, cities create more than resilient edges—they shape collective urban futures that reflect humanity's capacity to adapt, collaborate, and thrive in harmony with the water that sustains life.

www.ingramcontent.com/pod-product-compliance
Lightning Source LLC
Chambersburg PA
CBHW052139270326
41930CB00012B/2952